I0569100

THE UNMASKED TRUTH

TIP Press, LLC.
www.theilluminatedpath.org/tip-press
tippress@theilluminatedpath.org

ISBNs: 979-8-218-61341-9 (paperback) 979-8-218-43767-1 (ebook)

Front cover photo courtesy of Eberhard Grossgasteiger/Unsplash
Cover and book design by Molly Mortimer, Mayfly book design

Library of Congress Catalog Number: 2025901715
First Printing: 2025

Finally, Clear & Practical Insight!

THE UNMASKED TRUTH

How dark energy can affect your life
& what can be done about it

RICHARD HAMM

To my wife: I have such a depth of gratitude for my wife. She has proven to me why our closest relationships are in fact sacred. She has been open-minded and gracious as I have sought to grow in consciousness and spiritual knowing. She has helped to provide comfort to which I could return in the midst of what at times seemed like chaos. There is a reason our spirits resonate so deeply with each other. I love you more than words can express. I am so grateful. Do you want to go on another adventure?

To My Dear Friends: My knowing about the subject of this book (and many other subjects) would not have been possible without the direct personal involvement of my good friends (and coaches) Paul, Alice, and Hope. I can't tell you the depth of my appreciation for each of you and the role you have played in my personal growth and development. Won't it be fun to high-five and compare notes on the other side? Thank you, thank you, thank you—three times for emphasis.

CONTENTS

INTRODUCTION

Welcome

I'm so glad you picked up this book! You are at a point on your path of spiritual growth and development that this information is especially important to you. How do I know that? You are holding it in your hands. You would not have attracted this material if you were not ready for it. I'm honored to be on this path with you!

The information herein offers you the ability to avoid unseen obstacles to your spiritual growth and development that may otherwise be unknown. Without this knowledge, it is very possible to continue to feel bad and unknowingly be derailed.

You are not just a passenger on this physical journey. You are the pilot of your life. It is important for you to be empowered with this knowledge so that you are comfortable navigating it as you continue along your path.

The Context of This Material

I was a professional corporate pilot for a number of years and prior to that a flight instructor. Whenever I would fly passengers, it was my top priority for them to feel safe and comfortable. I would plan way ahead to avoid turbulence, abrupt maneuvers, and generally do all I could to minimize upset. I would have plenty of refreshments aboard to help ensure they had a good experience.

On the other hand, I also taught a number of people how to fly. As a flight instructor my role changed significantly. As a flight instructor, my job was to ensure that my student(s) knew how to handle all aspects of aviation including successfully navigating a number of emergency situations.

They would learn to react and recover from engine failures in all phases of flight, instrument failures, especially critical during instrument meteorological conditions, communications failures, lost procedures, recovery from unusual attitudes and other aerodynamic upsets like stalls (when airflow breaks from the wings due to the critical angle of attack being exceeded), and avoiding or recovering from the resultant spin(s).

All of this emergency training required me to make my students quite uncomfortable at times. They had to actually experience and recover from these multiple upsets routinely. Yet soon, each became quite comfortable within that environment because they had experienced the various situations so many times, they became confident in how to handle them.

So, while this material may feel a bit uncomfortable initially, I assure you that by staying with it you too will learn how to respond to this *actually quite common* "upset" that is experienced in our physical earth plane environment.

The Scope of This Book

Please know that in order to narrow the scope of this book, I had to make an assumption that you have a level of "energetic, metaphysical, or spiritual" knowledge. However, I have also **bold italicized** words and phrases that could be unfamiliar. Definitions or descriptions to them can be found in the glossary.

So What Is It?

What are we talking about here? Well, one of the greatest challenges to all of us on the earth plane, especially to those on a **conscious spiritual path**, is that there is unseen "**dark energy**" or entities that oppose The Light. In my experience, they actively seek to dissuade, disempower, distract, scare, block, impose, sabotage, and otherwise do all they can to discourage you (putting it mildly) from your spiritual path.

To be clear, some call these entities "demons." I generally do not use this terminology due to the fear it can elicit. However, I want to mention the term here just so there is no ambiguity.

But good news! You just need knowledge to oppose their efforts; the reason for this book. You have the power and you are in control!

This book will give you the knowledge and the tools that you need so that you no longer feel vulnerable while proactively and positively keeping them at bay. You will learn their tactics and tools and will also learn how to remove them from your environment and even from your energy and physical bodies, should it become necessary.

It is my desire to teach everyone willing to listen so that not only will your personal life be one of joy and Light, but that our collective Light may continue to brighten on the earth plane.

If you feel more immediate help is necessary, you can find it at www.theilluminatedpath.org/support or www.rich hamm.com

CHAPTER ONE

BACKGROUND

So you may be wondering how in the world does one learn about "dark energy"? Well, not really by conscious choice. However, I believe that my *higher self* or *The Universe* has assisted me in gaining the necessary knowledge and understanding by having many, many personal experiences.

My Initial Experiences

In 2008, I was barely a year into my conscious path of spiritual growth and development when I started to work with a life coach, Paul, who taught me a lot about energy. My desire was to feel better.

I was shocked to learn that unresolved energies significantly contribute to feeling bad. I learned how many humans stuff these energies into their bodies in order to avoid the uncomfortable feeling(s) created in the moment.

Among many other things, Paul taught me how to resolve these uncomfortable feelings that over time accumulate and contribute to covering the natural Peace that underlies everyone's experience.

After several months, he suggested we include Alice, a "psychic medium" in our meetings. Alice happened to be his neighbor. I was non-committal, yet he would suggest a meeting every few weeks.

As a child, I remember asking my father about friends who were playing with **Ouija boards**. My father, an Episcopal priest, quite seriously and sternly cautioned for me to stay clear of those kinds of activities because of the potential of contacting dark energy. (*I'm convinced I chose my parents due to their focus. Choosing a priest as a father is now telling for me.*)

His admonition stayed with me into my early 40's, my age at this time. Yet I trusted Paul and I was also getting used to considering new ideas and experiences. Finally, I reluctantly agreed to this meeting.

My Buddy

About six months prior to the meeting with Paul and Alice, a very good friend of mine took his own life. Michael was someone I had taught to fly, and we and our wives went on to have many adventures together. He was one of the most authentic, kind, and generous people I have ever known.

He and his wife owned an electrical business they had started from nothing and soon were building houses and developing real estate. When I first met him, I recognized him as the kind of business owner I aspired to be should I become one someday.

About twelve months prior to Michael taking his own life, he had heart surgery to repair a defect. Soon after, he went into a deep depression that he was unable to escape; more on that story later. But this has relevance to Paul, Alice, and my initial meeting together and what we would later learn.

Our Meeting

I had felt that my buddy Michael had been trying to get my attention for several weeks; like he had a message for me. So I was curious if he would "come through" during our meeting with Alice.

Sure enough, right from the beginning, Alice said "someone is here," and described my friend, his sense of humor, and other specific characteristics. We talked flying and discussed some of the adventures we had been on. Alice thought she was seeing a daughter connected to Michael, but from her description it was clear to me it was his wife.

At some point, Michael's mood changed from his normal jovial self. Alice said, "He's crying and is trying to apologize for something." (At this point Alice did not know that he had taken his own life.) His sudden passing hit me and many of his friends hard. I remember being surprised by my level of grief.

I was able to assure Michael that I had already forgiven him and loved him all the same. I remember feeling saddened that I wasn't available during the time that he was struggling. I was dealing with my own issues and could hardly focus on anything else.

Alice Saw Something

Soon Alice was joining Paul and I during all of our coaching sessions. Paul would receive spiritual or non-physical information using *applied kinesiology* or *muscle testing* and would guide and help me resolve all kinds of energetic issues that I was experiencing.

For reference, when I initially started these coaching sessions, my *vibration*, on the scale of one to nineteen, a one being the highest correlating with Love and Peace, mine was at a seventeen, correlating with despair. That is to say, I had quite a lot to clear *energetically*.

Alice was able to describe what was going on nonphysically as these things were resolved. So not only did I feel the resolution, I (we) received a deeper level of understanding of how things were working nonphysically due to the descriptions Alice was able to provide. It was so fascinating and enlightening!

We laughed a lot and I remember feeling that our meetings were magical. My personal "feel good" was drastically improving and I was learning so much. I began to hold a higher vibration for longer periods of time between meetings. It was a time full of wonder.

We had touched on the idea of "evil" a few times over the course of our meetings, and I remember being a little surprised that both Paul and Alice generally felt that the root of all evil was in the heart of man as opposed to being an outside influence. I wondered if they were right, though I was taught evil was an outside force. However, at this time a lot of what I had believed was shifting so I remained uncertain and open to the Truth.

During one of our sessions, Paul was "checking around the most optimal" thing to work on that day. I don't even recall specifically what it was. But we proceeded with it while Alice provided narration for us about what was happening as we resolved various ***energies***. I noticed at one point she stopped sharing what she was seeing. I thought it was a little odd, as she was typically so engaged and provided excellent descriptions during our conversations. I figured maybe she just wasn't getting anything interesting to share so didn't think much of it.

The next day, Paul called me. The conversation went something like this: "Hey Rich, Paul, how are you doing?" "Good Paul, what's happening?" I said. "Well, I wanted to talk to you about our session yesterday." "Yeah?" I said. "Well (*slight pause*), Alice saw something." He continued, "She saw a little demon guy floating around you. He was just a little guy, not really much to worry about."

Apparently Alice wanted to digest what she had seen and discuss it with Paul privately before they disclosed it to me. I would later learn this was the first "demon" she had ever seen. "Ahh, so *that* was the reason she stopped talking during our previous session," I thought. Much later I would joke with Paul about that conversation, how he had to break it to me that I had, "Just a smidge of evil, nothing to worry about." (Say this in your best English Monty-Python accent. It's hilarious.)

That next week, we discussed this more in depth. Alice described what she had seen; a little demon guy, small horns, tail, scaly and "a beautiful color of brown." I remember being surprised that she described this demon guy as "beautiful" anything. She felt it was just "watching me."

While I admit to feeling a little concerned, I was not overwhelmed by fear. I just felt it was interesting information, yet I believe all of our paradigms were shifting. Little did I know where this would lead.

Spiritual Surgery

Around this time, I was also reading every spiritual book that I came across. Jack, (*Jack Canfield*), Eckhart, (*Eckhart Tolle*), Deepak, (*Deepak Chopra*) and Esther and Jerry (*Esther & Jerry Hicks & Abraham*) were just a few who I felt I was on a first name basis with as I read and reread their books to ensure I had absorbed the material. Every spare minute I had I was either reading or listening to audio books.

I had made great strides in feeling better with Paul and Alice's help. I was also seeing positive shifts in my daily experiences as I learned to focus on what I wanted while minimizing any opposite distraction. Synchronicities were so common that I was no longer surprised when they occurred.

Besides feeling better personally, our company, one of the reasons for my despair that helped to launch me on my conscious spiritual path, was showing significant signs of improvement in overall revenue, cash flow, and profitability.

I was meeting with Paul and Alice two to three times a week during this time. During one of our sessions, Paul had located an area in my chest that needed attention. When looking, Alice described that area as appearing black. I remember saying, "That doesn't sound good."

As Alice continued to watch, Paul suggested I use the "core" technique to start to resolve the energy. (The core technique is when one "looks" or focuses attention directly into the "core" of the problem area.)

As I focused directly at the right side of my chest, Alice said it seemed like this was some kind of "entity," but she wasn't getting a lot of detail. For some reason, I asked if I needed to ask it to leave. She wasn't sure, but between her and Paul, they agreed I should ask. So I asked whatever this was to leave; that I had appreciated whatever it had taught me, but it was time for it to go.

Alice said that as I was talking, this black blob turned into an angry face, but nothing further happened immediately. Generally, when identifying a "trapped energy" it would typically resolve quite quickly, like within a few seconds. So, this was uncommon to not have the issue resolve quickly.

Then Alice said, "Oh, it looks like we are going to have a ***spiritual surgery***. (Interestingly I had just read a book about John of God, where spiritual surgeries were described. I was quite interested to experience it and honored to have the attention and help.

Alice described a team of spirits with shiny, silver-type medical instruments that went to work removing this dark entity. She described how they literally cut and pried it out of the affected area. It took five to ten minutes. Afterward, I could feel a slight ache in the area that actually lasted a few weeks.

I was so humbled as Alice described Mother Teresa joining us to help care for the surgical area after the surgery. She then described how the area was, "filled with Light." I can still pinpoint exactly where that area is in my chest today.

This was my (our) first experience with dark energy / entities actually residing in the body. I had no idea that I had *THAT* going on. I was interested to see what difference having it removed would make in my life. I remember feeling so honored and elated for the help from the "***Good Guys***."

This was such a significant event that I had to share it with my wife. I wasn't sure how she would respond. But to her credit, she listened and didn't "freak out," though I could tell she wasn't sure. I understood. This was such a personal experience it would be hard to relate to it without experiencing it yourself. However, I was thankful to be able to share it with someone.

With the removal of this entity, *along with the other **energetic work** we had done,* I found my personal ***energetic vibration***, or general "feel good," had significantly improved in a very short time.

While no surgeries were involved thereafter, during subsequent sessions I would have other "entities" removed, this time by Archangel Michael. Thus began my (our) relationship with him.

We learned that while it is Archangel Michael's mission to help protect us, he couldn't always see the dark entities without the help of them being pointed out first by either Paul (using muscle testing) or Alice (by seeing them in her mind's eye). Apparently, the vibrational difference between the two is so great that the low energy beings are many times invisible to angels and other spirits from The Light who vibrate at a much higher frequency.

Drive-Bys

Between our sessions, I started to experience something else. I would be going about my daily business and out of nowhere feel a strong sense of dread or foreboding; like something terrible was about to happen.

I would feel terribly threatened, fearful, and panicked. I had no idea what was going on. Sometimes these episodes would last a few seconds up to half an hour. I would always remain as totally present as possible until the feeling passed. Thankfully I was able to explore these experiences I was having with Paul and Alice.

One of the earliest experiences I had happened one day when I was hanging a small picture in our master bathroom for my wife. She was telling me where she wanted the picture hung and once decided, with my wife standing next to me, I drove the nail into the wall using my hammer.

As I did this, out of the blue I had a very clear image appear in my mind's eye of the hammer I was using harming my wife. I was shocked and taken aback. I knew this wasn't my desire. (*At this time, I didn't share this experience with my wife. I just finished the project and put everything back away as quickly as possible.*) However, I was ready for answers the next time Paul, Alice, and I met.

As we explored this and other experiences, Alice said it looked like I was "under attack" from these demon guys during these times. We were all piecing together the hierarchy and the organization. She could now tell if a dark entity was more powerful if it was wearing a cape. I pictured the capes she described as one like **Dracula** would wear. I now called these entities "***bad guys***."

Side note: While I have come to call these dark entities "bad guys," at the time I was surprised to learn that they too are welcomed back into the Light or The Kingdom of Heaven any time they choose to return. God or Source's Love truly is unconditional! Continue reading to learn what happens should they choose not to return to The Light.

I also came to call these attacks, "**drive-bys**." Though still feeling threatened, I began to get better at discerning where the threat was coming from. Because of our experience with Archangel Michael, any time I felt I was under attack, I started asking him to join me and I'd point out where I was feeling the threat. Usually within a few short seconds I would feel relief and calm.

We learned a lot about these bad guys during this time. Inquiring why I was the subject of so much attention, the answer was, "because your Light is becoming brighter." I remember Paul saying, "Really, it's a compliment that you are attracting attention. It shows you are improving." I appreciated that perspective.

During another session, I was describing the drive-bys to Paul and Alice again, something they had become accustomed to hearing. Right at that moment, I sensed a bad guy behind me and to my right. Alice "looked" and said, "Oh yeah, that's a big bad guy with a cape." She went on to describe Jesus appearing and standing between me and the bad guy, kind of staring the bad guy down. After just a short time, the bad guy left. It may sound unbelievable, but at this point it was common for Jesus to join us during our sessions. I was feeling like I really knew him.

I took several things from that experience. I wasn't alone,

I was indeed being heard and my **Spirit Team** really was responding to these threats. And I thought how amazing it was that Jesus could stand and stare this guy down. Yet, he indicated I (we) could do the same thing. I felt like he was acting like a big brother; protecting me when necessary but mostly guiding me and allowing me to learn.

These drive-bys continued like an onslaught for over five years. It was typical to have attacks three to five times per day. However, this experience has helped me to hone my abilities. I am now able to quickly identify and discern threats. Archangel Michael is always faithfully available (*to me and to you*) any time assistance is needed. I'm so thankful to him! I feel like we have become close friends.

More on Archangel Michael and his assistance in Chapter Seven.

Hope

Going back to my buddy Michael who I was reunited with the first time Alice joined Paul and me, I was glad to be able to introduce his wife Hope to Alice.

I actually waited six months before I told Hope about Alice because I was concerned she would think I was crazy. It was actually my wife who brought it up to Hope initially. My trepidation was unfounded as she was totally open to the idea of mediums being able to connect with those who have crossed over. I was so relieved.

Though the details are for her to share should she ever desire, with Alice's help, she and Michael were able to work through much grief and unfinished business since his passing.

I Know Why!

One day I returned home from one of my coaching sessions with Paul and Alice. I had started to teach myself piano and I was working on learning a simple song as I recall. As I was playing, I had a sudden realization or knowing that just hit me. The reason my buddy Michael had taken his own life was that he had been under the influence of a bad guy.

The next day, as if on cue, Hope called me. She had just been with Alice. She said, "I know why Michael took his own life. He was under the influence of a big bad guy." All I said was, "I know." "Of course you do," she said. She went on to describe how the bad guy had entered undetected when Michael was having his heart surgery months earlier.

Most Wanted

One day, after years of having these experiences and being tired of the assault by the bad guys, I asked Alice (again) if she could see any further information why I was such a target. She "looked" and said that I was on the bad guy's "most wanted list." I asked if there were any way that I could be removed from it now. I remember her saying, "I'm glad you asked." And then she described how a hand appeared and pulled a thumbtack from the list that was hanging on a board and it fell to the floor.

Since then, while I still experience drive-bys on occasion, by maintaining awareness and routinely clearing my energetic body and environment, this has become much less of an issue; reduced by about 85 percent.

Interestingly, relatively recently I have found the bad guy's tactics have changed with me. Now instead of the higher-level bad guys threatening, the harder to detect lower-level bad guys are now more prevalent around me. They sometimes come in multiples to which I have recently learned amplifies their overall power. (One little bad guy plus another little bad guy's energy equals the cumulative power of a larger, potentially mid-level entity's energy.)

Chapter Summary

These are just a few of the seemingly hundreds, likely thousands of experiences that I have had with these guys. Yet it gives you a sense that the knowledge in this book has been attained through direct personal experience. I believe that I set up my current life's experiences so that I could become fully proficient at personally dealing with dark entities.

By understanding all about them, not only am I able to have a different experience in this lifetime, I can also share my understanding with you so you too can minimize their effect on your life! With awareness, each of us can significantly minimize their impact on our lives.

CHAPTER TWO

THE ORGANIZATION & WHO IS AFFECTED

When I first learned about these dark entities, I felt righteously indignant. I couldn't believe we had these disincarnate bad guys just roaming around the earth plane wreaking havoc wherever and upon whoever they desired. What is worse is they have such an advantage since they are invisible to most.

Stay encouraged; we have significant natural protection. Just feeling good and maintaining a high *vibration* is one of the most significant protections. Also, each of us can learn to resolve any issues created by these guys, the purpose of this book.

But along this journey I have asked about the origin of bad guys and why they seek to cause harm (How exhausting it would be to begin with!) Alice shared the image she received when I asked these questions.

Envision a platform of angels up in heaven with a presenter or "speaker" at the front. Alice said it looked like the angels in the back of the gathering started to think that they could do better with the particular issue(s). She described that as they continued to focus on what they perceived as their ability to "do it better," they would continue to move further and further backward until at some point they would "fall off" the platform; literally, the idea of a "fallen angel." Apparently, the personal ego of the angel/entity is the driving force behind them "falling from heaven."

After further contemplating the experience of a fallen angel, I now realize that angels too can choose to experience heavier energy and "ego" much like humans. When that happens, their vibration drops and they "fall from heaven" to a more dense environment; the earth plane.

Checking further around this understanding with Alice, the information she received concurred and added just like humans, angels also have to be aware of their personal vibration. I had wrongly assumed that once on the other side and being fully immersed in Unconditional Love that one would never stray from that high vibration. Yet apparently that was inaccurate and confirms that things really are "as above, so below."

Another way to consider this is on the earth plane we experience duality: love and fear, light and darkness, black and white, good and bad. It seems that this isn't limited to just human experience but also to that of spirits. Just like humans can be focused on either Love and Light or darkness and fear, so too can spirits enter the world of duality.

Light on one end would correlate to angels, masters, and loved ones who positively assist us. On the other side, darkness, fear, and ego would correlate to the spirits that we experience as "dark energy," "demons," or "bad guys" who seek to make our path more difficult while feeling like they amplify themselves in the process.

I wondered with Alice if these guys had ever considered that if they ever had their way and totally destroyed humanity that they would be left with nothing to do. The information she received was that they gave their actions no thought nor considered the broader ramifications. It was all about ego; they want to be recognized and to gain power within the organization.

It was comforting to learn that the bad guys would never destroy humanity. The "power ratio" between Light and dark may ebb and flow a bit, but darkness would not fully take over.

Hierarchy

It seems there is a hierarchy in the "dark energy" world. They can have a range of personal power; high or low it seems, dependent on their experience.

I have noticed the "high level" entities can be felt much more readily as their personal negative vibration is so much stronger. Less powerful "little guys" can go undetected more easily because their energy is not so strong and is more easily disguised.

Who They Affect

So who do these guys really affect? Well, they likely affect all of us on the earth plane in one way or another. Just look at all the violence in the world for instance.

Yet it can be much more personal than that. Any little "bad habit" can have outside influence. And personal struggles and traumas can be significantly amplified by these guys.

Worse, due to the nature of their tactics (*discussed more in depth later*), much of the time it is difficult to determine that the root cause or amplification of the problem is due to outside, negative dark energy that has been disguised as your own.

Get Off of Her!

One night, years ago, I awoke to hearing my wife sobbing uncontrollably. I asked her what was wrong, but she would not wake up. Knowing what I know, I started to "look" energetically at what might be going on.

In my mind's eye, I saw a red sinewy demon guy jumping up and down on my wife's shoulders. Without thinking I said, "You get off of her!" while asking Archangel Michael to remove it. I watched as he was removed and within thirty seconds my wife was sleeping peacefully.

This is an example of a bad guy just generally causing grief and disruption much like a vandal would damage property; for no particular reason.

Side Note: This is the one time I have asked for the removal of a dark entity without the knowledge of the person I was working with. It was quite automatic to protect my wife and I didn't even think about it until the situation was over. However, I shared this with my wife the next morning so she had full awareness. Please know that it is not a good idea to have a bad guy removed without the knowledge of the person for multiple reasons, explained in Chapter Seven.

While each of us is likely affected at some point in our lives, there are certainly situations that draw more attention.

Light Becoming Brighter

Some may attract more attention than others. As mentioned in the previous chapter, if your Light is bright or becoming brighter, it is possible you will draw more interest. This is not a reason to stop pursuing The Light however! Stay the course! What you need will appear when you need it. This book may be one of your resources.

As mentioned previously, as my personal vibration improved and my Light became brighter, this is when I first was aware of their efforts. However, I must say though that, as described earlier, I had been living with several entities prior to my conscious pursuit of spiritual growth and development, very likely amplifying my feelings of despair. They were removed over a short span of time while working with Paul and Alice. So one can be a target for other reasons discussed below.

Influence & Power

Those who have more influence and power can be more focused upon, such as heads of state, leaders of organizations, and others with a broader impact. This is one good reason to pray for our leaders and ask for their energetic protection.

Adolf Hitler is probably the most extreme example of a leader overtaken by dark entities. However, I'm quite confident that much if not all of the daily "evil" perpetuated on humanity is influenced by dark entities.

Drugs

Others who have drug and alcohol addictions may also have more vulnerability as they open themselves up to these energies by losing their personal awareness.

This was evident one day when I received a call from someone I was working with. I could tell by her energy as we spoke and the feeling I had in my stomach that her vibration/energy was significantly low. She was making really odd remarks and ended our phone conversation by saying something like, "It's okay, I've had a good life." I was highly concerned as I felt that was a suicidal statement, so I decided to drive to her house as fast as I could.

When I arrived, I could tell this person was out of sorts. I asked if I could look to see what was going on "energetically," and after a few minutes she agreed. Finally, she confided in me that, she was hearing voices and they are, "Talking so mean to me." Then following a fairly rational conversation, she would flip in a split second and get really angry with me and start yelling at me nose to nose.

I was able to **hold my focus** and found out this person indeed had a powerful dark entity bothering her. I asked Archangel Michael to remove it and she calmed down. Then out of the blue she would start again either complaining about "hearing voices" or being really angry and yelling at me again.

Again, I would check (mostly using muscle testing at this point) to discern what was going on. Sure enough, another entity would be influencing her, and I'd ask for its removal, and she would calm down again.

At one point this person asked, "How much time do I have *before I start hearing voices again.*" I told her she could be at peace forever if she desired, and assured her we would get beyond this. Then another guy would jump in and off we'd go again. While feeling a little overwhelmed, I stayed with it. I was shocked at how fast they were coming in!

We, Archangel Michael and I, probably cleared eight to ten entities in a two-hour period. Finally, the bad guys must have figured out that whoever attacked this person was going to be identified and removed. The attacks finally stopped.

Side note: When an entity is removed, they no longer are able to harm another, so I believe that was likely the reason why they finally stopped; so they could "live to fight another day." More on what happens when an entity is removed in Chapter Seven.

Later I found out this person had been under the influence of a strong drug that had opened her up to these lower vibrational beings. Thankfully, she is well beyond this issue now and doing very well.

However, this was a profound experience for me. It deepened my understanding of how dark entities prey on vulnerabilities and demonstrated how they can orchestrate coordinated "attacks" if desired.

As noted earlier, even those undergoing anesthesia may be more vulnerable due to not having their personal awareness as my buddy Michael experienced. *With this knowledge, when I know of someone who is having surgery, I ask for their space to be cleared in pre-op, in transit to the operating room, in the operating room, and in the recovery room. I also ask for angels to stand watch for them throughout the procedure. Then I closely monitor that person for any potential issues while they recover over the course of time. Avoidance and protection will be more fully discussed in Chapter Eight.*

Illness

Some may also be more vulnerable due to lower physical energy caused by illness. One simply can be an easier target because during illness focus is drawn into the physical body and overall awareness can be reduced or lost. It is also harder to notice a difference in feeling when one is already feeling physically bad.

Chronic Thinking

Chronically thinking about dark energy can even open the door. I have to say, when I first started to experience their more overt tactics, I was quite overwhelmed and fearful and was constantly worried and thinking about these guys. Then I learned early on that even chronically thinking about them can be an opening for them. So I did all I could to soothe myself to stop the chronic thinking.

This actually makes sense if you think about it from a Law of Attraction standpoint. Being focused and worried about keeping bad guys away actually draws them closer. It is very similar to being focused on "not having money," as that thought and corresponding vibration draws more of the experience of "not having money" to you. So in the case of thought, simply not focusing on them at all is helpful.

Fear

Keep in mind fear in any form can create more vulnerability. So notice fearful thoughts and avoid fearful activities like horror films. Yes, these movies lower your personal vibration (unless you are very practiced at *holding your center*.) I actually find these movies repulsive. They support the "bad guys" and give them more opportunity to influence people. For me, I avoid all activities that lower my personal vibration, including watching scary movies. Fear of any kind can allow an opening. It is not a mistake that horror films are a popular genre.

Lower Vibrational Attitudes & Beliefs

Anything that is held as a lower vibrational nature can be taken advantage of by the "bad guys" and amplified. Some examples include but are not limited to intolerance, judgement, superiority, inferiority, unworthiness, helplessness, hopelessness, shame, bigotry, guilt, jealousy, resentment, insecurity, despair, and bitterness, just to name a few.

An Easy Target

Bad guys are opportunists. If a person has minimal awareness and is generally living life by happenstance, reacting to conditions and generally not feeling good (having a lower relative vibration) as many of us have, they can be an easier target.

Seeking Attention

Finally, and as unbelievable as it is to me, there are humans who seek the attention of dark energy. They literally open themselves up to being used by them in some manner. This is of course directly opposed to our mutual intent to focus on Love and Light.

Chapter Summary

Bad guys are fallen angels who have lowered their vibration by pursing ego objectives and literally "fell from heaven" into our lower vibrational environment, the earth plane. There is a spectrum of dark entities both in strength and power that can affect us in multiple ways. There are several reasons one may become a target. For those pursuing a spiritual path, your Light becoming brighter is likely the biggest reason.

CHAPTER THREE

TACTICS

How Bad Guys Affect Humans

Bad guys can affect humans in several ways. They can simply color the environment, they can "reach in" to the **aura** or body without fully entering it, they can enter the auric field and reside there or they can fully enter into the body. Entities can disguise their presence by matching a person's feeling tone (sadness, anxiety, depression, etc.) or mask themselves within the habits and dependencies we may already have.

Let's consider each tactic individually.

Environment

Have you ever noticed that some physical environments feel better or worse than others? This is due to their **energetic signature**. The energy of the area, location, or building is comprised of the collective "vibration" of its history and those that currently frequent it.

Pay attention to how buildings, airports, cities, and even states feel *"energetically."* If a certain locale feels especially heavy, that can be in part due to the heavier energy of bad guys in the area. By paying attention to how the energy of any given place feels, it can help you to determine if dark energy may be present.

This isn't just limited to the buildings or establishments where you might guess heavier energy would be present. It can happen anywhere, even churches!

Mom's Experience

When I was in grade school, my father took a position as a mission priest in Montana. He served three different Episcopal churches in three different towns. Each parish on its own was not big enough to support a full-time pastor.

Every Sunday, my father would have three services and I would join him as his "acolyte," maybe more commonly known by some as his "altar boy." We would start at 8:00 a.m. in our hometown of Sheridan. After the first service, we would drive to Ennis, a town about forty-five minutes away in his Jeep CJ-5 for a 10:00 a.m. service. On our way back, we would stop midway in Virginia City to have one more service at 11:30 a.m. (St. Paul's church in Virginia City was the oldest church in the Diocese of Montana.) We'd finally make it home around one or 1:30 p.m. and we would walk into our home, greeted by the wonderful smells of a meal my mom had prepared for Sunday dinner.

Years later my mom and I were talking about spiritual things and reminiscing about our experience in Montana.

She explained how at one point she noticed the church in our hometown felt uncomfortable. Initially it was not clear to her why.

She explained how on a quiet day she decided to walk the short distance over to the church to investigate. The entry door to the church was in the rear and it opened directly into the sanctuary. The church roof had a high pitch with exposed crossbeams throughout.

She explained that as she walked through the door she happened to look up and was stunned by what she saw. She told me, "On the crossbeams were three demons sitting there side by side." She explained how they were as clear to her as she was looking at me that day. She had just found the reason for her discomfort.

She explained how she got out of their quickly and later talked to my dad about it. Ultimately, they asked for (spiritual) help so these guys would not harm anyone. It seemed this was new territory for them.

Side note: You see what I mean when I said how I'm convinced I chose my parents based on who they were/are and their focus? I'm so thankful to them for their guidance and example!

Know that it is very easy to clear physical space. Keep reading to learn how.

Disguise & Amplification

When it comes to troubling humans, dark entities are opportunists. As mentioned briefly above, one of their most prolific strategies is to "jump in" on an energy or emotion that is already active within the person.

For instance, if someone is angry, the entity can disguise itself by matching the exact same feeling tone of that anger being experienced, thereby entering undetected. They can literally do this with any negative human emotion. Feeling sad? Then sadness can be the entry point. Any heavier human emotion can be an entry point.

After entry, many times the dark energy will significantly amplify the "entry" feeling or emotion. The affected person can feel like the depth of the negativity is totally due to their own issue(s) when in fact the feeling is being significantly amplified by a dark entity.

A Recent Experience

This is an experience I had just a few weeks ago *at the time of writing this book*. While I have gotten quite good at **maintaining my center**, I am still human and something happened where I reacted and felt mildly frustrated. On a scale of one to ten, ten being high, my frustration was around a two. I dealt with this (*human interaction*) issue and was able to resolve the situation quite rapidly. I then continued working and didn't think much else about it.

On the drive home that evening, I noticed I still was experiencing mild frustration, not at the specific event, but just in general. I arrived home and I felt mildly irritated about petty things. Finally, my wife said to me, "You got a bug?" That's what she now calls bad guys.

With the experience I have, I still hadn't thought to check to see if I had something "energetic" going on. I checked and sure enough, I had a low-level bad guy in my aura around my heart area. I asked Archangel Michael to remove it and I was back to normal within just a few seconds.

This is how deceptive and disguised they can be. The entity had exactly matched my original mildly frustrated feeling. *The clue I was experiencing an influence was the frustration continued for a significant time beyond the original situation and was noticed later around other unrelated events.*

Progression

From my experience, it seems, generally speaking, that bad guys enter the **aura** matching the general feeling tone or active negative emotion of the person. They then begin to amplify that emotion and potentially cause other negativity while working their way into the body. After they are in, they can dwell there undetected by those unaware.

Hidden or Masked

Dark entities can also hide and mask themselves to make it more difficult to be noticed. I have generally found this when detecting them within my own or another person's body, but I have also found some do this in the outside environment as well.

It is not clear to me why all entities do not hide and mask themselves as it frankly seems to be an effective tactic. Perhaps it is a skill that a more advanced entity must learn in order to do this, but that is total speculation.

Hidden/masked entities can be harder to detect by those assisting others. However, the person helping just needs to check if anything is "hidden or masked." Interestingly, just by checking "hidden or masked" exposes the entity. But one must remember to ask that important question.

See more about detection in Chapter Six and removal in Chapter Seven.

Reaching In

Dark entities can also "reach in" to your personal space without fully entering your aura or body. I have identified this on a number of occasions. This is done just to disturb and distract the person. It's like picking on a younger sibling when you know they are sensitive about something specific.

For instance, if a person has some sort of a "trigger," let's say the feeling of general insecurity, a bad guy can reach in and create that exact feeling within you. To the unaware person, this can start an unhelpful thought loop that continues that feeling. Mission accomplished.

I believe the other reason for reaching in is that it is less risky for the entity as they are able to retreat rapidly without detection if necessary. In other words, if you have become skilled at noticing bad guys then they may "reach in" instead of taking the risk of entering the aura or body and being caught. There is more on what happens when entities are caught in Chapter Seven.

Brute Force

I have also experienced these guys trying to enter my physical body with brute force; no disguise at all.

One night, when all of this was fairly new to me, I was driving home from one my daughter's musical performances.

Midway home I felt this sense of foreboding and dread; like something awful was about to happen. I was now experienced enough to know this was dark energy that was around me.

I continued driving while doing all I could to keep the entities at bay. I literally felt like I was being surrounded by a pack of wolves and I would deflect whichever one would approach or attack me at any given time.

At one point, I literally felt like one was jumping on me trying to enter my body through my shoulders. Finally, it occurred to me to ask Archangel Michael for help. Asking Archangel Michael for help stopped the attack immediately. I was so grateful and relieved. As mentioned, there will be more about resolution and removal in Chapter Seven.

Dependencies

Entities can also move in undetected around dependencies or habits that a person has formed and then strongly encourage that negative behavior. I have seen entities amplifying the desire for drugs and alcohol for instance. They can also jump in on sex, smoking, gambling, eating, and really any human activity that can become unhealthy or extreme. While not the specific subject of this book, interestingly, ***earth-bound spirits*** can do the same thing.

Chapter Summary

Dark entities are opportunists. Not only can they take advantage of the negative feelings and emotions that are being experienced by their target to match and mask their entry into their targets personal space, they can also enter by masking themselves as the same feeling tone as a craving and influence various habits and dependencies. Finally, they can affect the vibration or "feel good" of any physical environment.

CHAPTER FOUR

TOOLS

B esides affecting us directly, bad guys have other energetic tools that they can deploy to negatively affect our lives. In lieu of a bad guy directly causing the upset, it can use one of these tools instead.

Sometimes these devices are "installed," while other times we can "walk into them" like a booby trap. These tools are all energetic, yet designed with a specific intent.

The devices can negatively affect our energy or physical body in some way. They can also have fairly minor to quite significant impact. Different from the overall effect a dark entity has when residing in the auric field or body, in my experience, these devices cause a very specific localized problem.

It's not always clear where and when these devices are "picked up." However, other times one can determine the exact time it occurred. There is more about avoidance and protection in chapter Eight.

Control Device

One such energetic tool is a "control device," a name I have adopted from others to help describe it. A control device is an energetic mechanism that causes a very specific difficulty.

Like other actions taken by dark entities, it seems the only reason a control device is utilized is to be generally disruptive and to cause a distraction. As mentioned above, these devices can be set up like a "booby trap" and individuals can unknowingly walk right into them. (*It is possible to prevent this and protect yourself. See more on this in Chapter Eight.*) The best I can tell from my experience is these devices can also be targeted at a specific person directed by the dark entity.

When intuitively focusing on control devices with my mind's eye, they generally appear as a mechanical mechanism that causes a specific problem as described in the following examples. The representations received are surely metaphorical, depicted in terms I can understand.

Temporomandibular Joint (TMJ) Symptoms

One evening, I noticed slight pain in my jaw close to my ear. Initially I wasn't too concerned as I, like most, have experienced pain somewhere in my body that in a short time resolves itself.

However, this issue continued to worsen. Upon waking the next morning, I found it was hard to open my mouth just to brush my teeth. Over the next days, I started finding it difficult to eat. Soon the pain persisted as a dull ache when not moving my jaw at all.

When eating began to hurt so bad that it became a problem, I felt I may need to go see a doctor. Up until that point, I had not considered there was anything wrong other than something "physical."

However, before scheduling a medical appointment, for some reason, I decided to check, using muscle testing, to see if there was an energetic root cause for the pain. Sure enough, I was surprised to confirm that there was a control device affecting my jaw.

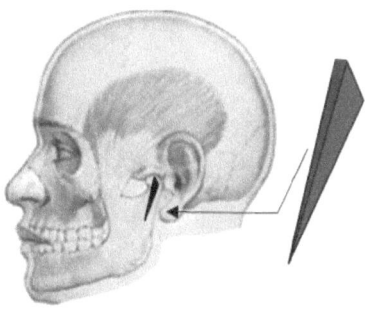

Rusty Shrapnel

I asked for Archangel Michael's help to remove the device and while that was underway I saw a picture in my mind's eye of a sharp pointed triangular piece of (what looked like) brownish rusty metal right in the joint of my jaw, close to my ear as pictured.

I felt about 85 percent of the pain resolved immediately when it was removed. I confirmed that the process of removal had been completed and asked that the area be filled with Love & Light. I then asked if there was anything further required to fully heal the affected area that it be done.

As always, I expressed much gratitude for the assistance that I had received.

My jaw ache went from severe pain, barely able to open my mouth to even eat, to comfortably eating and brushing my teeth within ten minutes or so. Since the bone and muscle were affected, it took another few days for all of the pain to subside, but the area rapidly healed.

Interestingly several years later, my good friend Hope (mentioned earlier in the book) called about pain in her jaw. She had been taking pain relievers and was (also) just about to go see a doctor. She was experiencing very similar symptoms as I described above.

I asked her if I could "look" for what might be going on energetically and she gave her consent. As soon as I focused, that same picture of the sharp piece of metal embedded in her jaw "flashed" in my mind's eye. I confirmed this information through muscle testing.

I shared with Hope my previous experience and the information I had received. Again, I asked Archangel Michael to remove the device. Joy indicated she felt a tingling, but no considerable relief in the moment. Based on my experience of having a significant reduction in pain immediately, I was surprised she wasn't feeling it.

I reconfirmed the device had been removed with muscle testing, then checked to see how long it would be for Hope to feel relief. I found it would be several hours before she would feel improvement. I let her know the information that I had received and asked her to check back if she didn't feel the expected resolution in the time indicated.

Several hours later, I got a call from Hope. She said she had decided to go to the store to pick up groceries. As she was shopping, she noticed significant relief. The timing seemed to be just about right. She, too, fully recovered quickly thereafter.

Severe Back Pain

Another example of a control device occurred during one of our family's Thanksgiving celebrations. We were having dinner at my parent's house and I noticed that I had a minor back pain while eating. I didn't think much of it at the time. As we relaxed after dinner, I found my back continued to worsen over the next few hours.

Finally, I went to stand from the chair I was sitting in but doubled over in pain. My core literally wouldn't support my weight. I knew I hadn't done anything to cause my back to hurt like this. So I "looked" for an energetic cause, using muscle testing to access information. Sure enough, I found a control device to be the root cause.

While I didn't get a visual of this particular device, I asked Archangel Michael to remove it and again I immediately felt relief. Within just a few moments, I was able to stand. But because my muscle had been affected, it took another few hours to fully resolve.

Sadness

Another interesting example is one I experienced when working with another person while resolving various energetic issues they were experiencing. They had commented on a feeling of sadness and general malaise. This time it was optimal to check this person's ***chakra energetic system***.

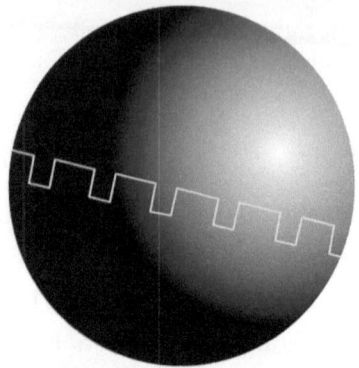

When I reached the heart chakra, in my mind's eye, I saw what I described as a black "clamshell" device totally surrounding this person's heart. It seemed to be made out of steel.

I asked Archangel Michael to remove this device and my client was grateful for the immediate relief and improvement in their personal energy and "feel good."

Energetic Spear

Over the years of identifying these devices, I began to characterize one of the tools used by dark energy as an "energetic spear." This was the result of a picture I received in my mind's eye when resolving a specific issue I was experiencing a number of years ago.

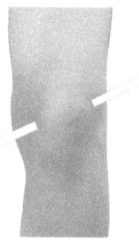

One day I was at the gym doing upper-body exercises. I sat down on a bench and noticed that all of a sudden, I had significant pain in my left knee. I thought I had just twisted it a little. I carried on with my workout. But when I went to get up, I found I could now hardly bend my knee. Just a few moments earlier I was totally fine.

Having enough experience at this point, I immediately looked for an energetic root cause. This time, I received an impression in my mind's eye of an "energetic spear" going right through my knee joint, extending a few feet on either side of the leg.

I asked Archangel Michael to remove it and within just a few seconds I was fine.

Hidden/Masked Control Device

Over the last several months (during the time of writing this book,) I would awake in the morning with a sharp pain in my mid-back muscle on the right side next to my spine. I believe the muscle is called the multifidus muscle.

Since I like to exercise with weights, when I have muscular pain, I don't always associate it with something "energetic." However, this pain became sharp over the next several weeks.

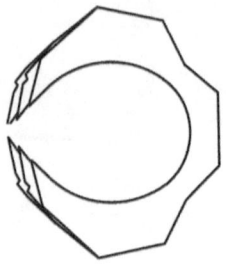

I explored the root cause of this problem multiple times without finding it. Experiencing the pain yet again, I decided to explore it another time to see if I had missed something.

I checked the following phrases with muscle tests: "The root cause is physiological," (like I had strained a muscle.) The answer was "no" to that. "The root cause is "energetic." Again, "no" to that too. "The issue is *past life* related"; also a "no."

I continued to check trapped emotion, subconscious programming, and multiple other potential root causes. All were a "no." (There is more on applied kinesiology or muscle testing coming up in Chapter Six.)

I didn't feel like this was "entity" related as I did not have any of the tell-tale signs and feelings of discomfort that are associated with them. However, it did seem like a control device, though my exploration never confirmed it.

For some reason, I decided to check if there were something "hidden or masked." My muscle test indicated a "yes" to that. I then checked "hidden or masked control device," and the answer was also "yes" to that.

While focusing on the area, I saw a picture in my mind's eye similar to a grapple, the teeth clenching the muscle in my back. I was thankful to have it removed and the sharp pain resolved immediately. It has not returned. (As mentioned, there is more on removal of both devices and dark energies in Chapter Seven.)

This was the first time I have experienced a hidden or masked *control device*. I was not aware those too could be hidden and masked. I'll remember to check that going forward.

Implants

An implant is very much like a control device. However, from my experience it seems the implant is "more personally directed" by the entity for a specific purpose and carries the additional symptom of being an energy drain.

I have found that when experiencing lower personal energy, if an implant is the root cause, once the implant is removed normal energy generally returns. This is accompanied by relief of any other physical or energetic symptom(s) the implant may have been causing.

Chapter Summary

Dark entities have energetic tools at their disposal that can be used to cause upset without their direct involvement once the device is placed. I have described just a few that I have found to be common. Yet there are likely infinite types of devices; whatever can be envisioned by the bad guy(s).

These devices cause localized issues and are removed using the same methods as having an entity removed as will be discussed in Chapter Seven.

CHAPTER FIVE

SYMPTOMS

You may be wondering how to determine if you (or potentially others) are experiencing dark energy's influence.

I'd like to start by sharing an actual experience I had some years ago. It's important to note this happened at least five to six years after I had learned about bad guys. I was quite experienced at identifying them and asking for their removal when this experience occurred.

The Basketball Game

Our son was a three-sport athlete growing up. We were always traveling for athletic events during this time. One weekend, he had a travel basketball tournament in a town a few hours away.

We set our clocks to get up early the next morning so that we could arrive in plenty of time for our son to warm up with the team prior to the first game of the day.

Unfortunately, we somehow miscalculated and were running behind schedule. Our son would still make warm ups if everything went right, but we were not as relaxed as we would have liked to have been. I was feeling frustrated about the whole situation.

As we arrived at the facility, our son ran inside to join the team. As it turned out, we had arrived in enough time for all to work out okay. However, I remained frustrated as we entered the facility and as we found our seats prior to the game.

We always loved watching our son play ball; while he was/ is a talented kid, what we really treasured was watching him do something that he loved. He and the whole team emanated natural enthusiasm, exuberance, and joy.

However, as the game got started I found I was not having that much fun watching at all. I felt quite agitated. I continued to relive the experience leading to me feeling frustrated. (Looking back, I was definitely in a thought loop.) I even started to blame my wife for the whole situation even occurring.

Our son played two games that morning. After the second game, we ran to a restaurant for lunch and then returned to the facility for the final game that day.

I dropped our son and my wife at the door and then went to park our vehicle. I was now just seething mad at my wife. I couldn't believe she would create this situation. (Notice it's ME keeping this going!)

I was so mad, instead of sitting with her and the other parents during the next game, I sat on the other side of the gym by myself. (My wife would later say the other parents were asking why I wasn't sitting with them.)

I was relieved the last game was done and I could finally get away from people. My anger was hard to conceal. I drove the two hours home not talking to my wife or son, the whole time feeling totally justified in my position and behavior.

Interestingly, during the drive home, I received a phone call from Alice and Hope; they happened to be together at the time. They asked if I could stop by Alice's house the next day as they felt I could use some help. I was surprised to get the phone call, but hesitantly agreed to stop by. (Generally, I would have been excited to get together. I remember noticing my resistance and reticence.)

That evening, I kept to myself. While the anger had lessened, I found it still was noticeable.

The next day I met with Alice and Hope. Paul may have been there too. We had been used to getting together and connecting with "The Kingdom," so this was not unusual. However, what was unusual is they felt I may be experiencing a bad guy influence. I remember thinking, "Maybe, but I usually pick up on these things." But I agreed to allow them to explore this for me.

I can't remember who did what, but essentially they did a "scan" of my energy to determine if there was an outside influence. I remember Alice saying, "Oh, sure enough. There is a big bad guy with a cape . . ." Later I would muscle test this entity on a scale of one to ten, with one being the lowest, it was a ten. It certainly was a "big bad guy."

She called on Archangel Michael to have it removed for me. As it was removed, I felt total relief, release, and resolution of the frustrated and angry feelings I was having. As I recall, it felt like a pressure totally releasing in my chest. Keep reading to learn what happens when entities are removed, discussed in Chapter Seven.

With all of the experience I had had, I couldn't believe I had been duped so easily! This was a huge lesson for me in many ways that I'll share shortly. But first, let's break down this actual experience.

Let's Break It Down

In an effort to explain how these entities work, let's consider this specific experience that I had at the basketball game. First, an opening was necessary for this entity to "slide in" to my energy body undetected.

I created this opening in my personal energy in the form of my mild frustration. (Note that lower vibrational emotions, feelings, or attitudes are necessary to create an opening. High vibrational feelings or states of being like Love would not create an opening but would actually create a layer of protection.) So the lower vibrational emotion created a crease that could be exploited.

I was also distracted and not as "tuned in" to my personal energy field given the hurried situation we were experiencing and the mild frustration I was feeling. I also was not pre-thinking to protect myself or my space prior to arriving at the venue.

Due to my lack of awareness and the opening that I had created, this big bad guy slid into my energy field undetected by matching the exact feeling tone of the mild frustration I was having. Then, in a very short time, he had significantly amplified those feelings and I believe encouraged me to blame my wife for the whole situation.

As hinted above, I also happened to be at an event with a significant number of people. Therefore, there was more potential for having bad guys hanging around just due to the density of humanity. (Entities may hang around and/or set up "booby traps" like control devices around large gatherings of people just because this gives them more targets and opportunity.)

It is also quite classic for dark energies to try to isolate their target. In this experience, in just three to four hours, I was already at the point of beginning to be isolated as demonstrated by my sitting alone on the other side of the arena.

I continued to become even more angry while sitting by myself and felt totally reasonable and justified in my anger and behavior the whole time. (In retrospect, my feelings and behavior were totally unreasonable.) I remember feeling the uncomfortable energy, almost a pain in my chest during this time, but I thought this was just from my own pent-up emotion. It all seemed like my energy.

Due to Alice and Hope's intervention (*I'm so thankful*), this was a relatively short-lived event. Yet I was flabbergasted that I could be influenced so significantly given my experience level.

My Lesson

This incident helped to shape my personal protection process discussed in Chapter Eight. It also significantly improved my personal awareness. Dark energy doesn't take time off. If there is an opportunity and they "want to," they will take advantage of those unaware. Therefore, maintaining awareness despite the situation is important. "Awareness" is discussed more in the upcoming chapter.

I'm also much more cautious of populated venues. Before entering a more populated area, event, market, etc., I actively set up protections as discussed in Chapter Eight.

Common Symptoms of Bad Guy Influence

The basketball story above gives you some idea of how bad guys gain access to one's *energetic field*. Yet, below you will find a more in-depth list of symptoms. Some, but not all, were experienced at the basketball game.

It's difficult to capture all possible symptoms that may be experienced with dark energy influence. Yet, from experience, I have found the following to be most common:

- General vibrational shift
- Amplification of negative emotion
- Negative emotion more commonly experienced
- Heavy or negative general outlook
- Ominous, gloomy, or threatening feeling
- You literally "feel" bad
- Racing negative thoughts
- Desire for isolation
- Compulsive behavior
- Inconsiderate of others
- Inexplicable worsening of pain over time

General Vibrational Shift

It is quite common to have a significant vibrational shift when under "bad guy" influence. For instance, one could go from feeling just fine to all of a sudden feeling depressed or sad or any lower frequency emotion. (Happy to sad would be a vibrational shift.)

It's also possible to notice the presence of dark energy in the environment just by noticing how it feels. This was described in Chapter One when I was meeting with Alice and Paul, I could sense a "big bad guy" behind me that Jesus stared down.

Amplification or Negativity Increase

Once a dark entity is within your personal space, they will likely begin to amplify the issue(s) that were the original entry point. As in the basketball story, mild frustration was amplified to significant anger quite rapidly.

Another way this can manifest is you can become just generally "more" of whatever the negative feeling is. With anger for example, you may not get angrier about the original specific situation, but you may just become generally more angry.

Insert any negative emotion and it works the same way. For instance, you may not be more fearful of something specific, but you might become generally more fearful of everything. Either way, there is a significant (rapid or gradual) shift from your general, normal state-of-being.

Also, if you notice that your negative feeling is significantly prolonged beyond your "normal" time of recovery, this can be another indicator of dark energy's influence.

Heavy or Negative General Outlook

Another potential symptom is having a generally negative outlook about everything with the feeling that it is difficult or impossible to change it.

Ominous/Gloomy/Threatening Feeling

I experienced an ominous, gloomy, or threatening feeling a lot during the time I was experiencing "drive-bys." It can be associated with the heaviness or negative outlook with the added feeling of being vulnerable and the added sense of dread, foreboding, anxiety, fear, and/or panic.

Feeling Bad

This is not the kind of feeling associated with emotion as above. This is literally the feeling in your body. You might notice an uncomfortable heaviness, tightness, or a subtle or sharp pain literally anywhere in the body. I have experienced pains in my head, shoulders, throat, chest, stomach (both solar plexus and sacral areas), and legs associated with bad guys.

Racing Negative Thoughts

Continuing with the basketball example, I could not stop thinking about the situation that made us late for the game and later how my wife "should have planned better." You can see how I could have dropped this thought loop immediately at any time; especially upon arrival when we found our timing was fine.

An untrained mind can certainly contribute to racing thoughts due to a lack of awareness. Yet if you have a relatively "trained mind," one might notice more negative racing thoughts that aren't generally part of your experience.

Also, the Law of Attraction assists in this persistence as negative thoughts draw more negative thoughts.

Desire for Isolation

I have noticed that dark energy's influence causes one to want to minimize contact with others. This is more than being introverted. It's the feeling of almost being repulsed by being around other people.

My buddy Michael, who took his own life, was very extroverted. Yet up to a year prior to his departure, it was difficult to get him to do anything to the point of being alarming.

Compulsive Behavior

We humans can develop bad habits that are not good for us. About any human activity can become detrimental: eating, exercise, sex, alcohol, and drugs for some examples. If it is decided that a particular activity is out of alignment with whom you want to be and you decide to stop, you may find a compulsion lying below the physical desire. It's possible that compulsion is associated with or being influenced by dark energy.

Inconsiderate

Those under the influence of dark energy may have little to no concern for others. They may be very self-absorbed and unable to see the bigger picture.

Pain Worsening Over Time

Especially in the instance of a control device or implant, you may experience a pain in the body gradually worsening from slight to being almost unbearable over a relatively short period of time; one to fourteen days.

This was mentioned previously in Chapter Two with both my and Hope's TMJ-type symptoms, as well as my severe back pain at our family Thanksgiving celebration.

Chapter Summary

This chapter sought to provide a general outline of symptoms that may be experienced when under the influence of dark energy. I encourage you to consider this as a potential root cause should you experience any of them. Your knowledge and awareness of these symptoms will be helpful in detection, discussed in the next chapter.

CHAPTER SIX

DETECTION

Methods of Detection

Now that you have more in depth knowledge of the signs or symptoms of dark energy's influences, let's discuss detection.

How do you actually detect dark energy? The method I have found to be most effective is using awareness. What do I mean by awareness? Awareness is noticing or being conscious of how your spirit feels in your body and any upsets to it.

Energetic Dissonance

Since you are on a spiritual path, chances are likely that you already have a relatively high vibrational state-of-being. (You generally feel good.)

By using your awareness, it is possible to notice the presence of heavier energy because dark entities vibrate at a much lower frequency. They just don't "feel good" and clash with your energy. You can notice that energetic dissonance; literally feeling the heaviness they emanate and from where it is coming from.

Some adjectives to describe these sensations are tightness (slight or significant), pain, cramping, or burning. While these sensations are not always caused by bad guys, when the feeling persists beyond what would feel reasonable, the location of that feeling may be a clue for where the dark energy is located.

Revisiting Chapter One Example

In Chapter One, I discussed a session with Paul and Alice where I felt a dark entity standing behind and to the right of me. Alice focused in that area and saw "a big bad guy" and watched as she described Jesus standing between me and it until the entity finally left.

Some adjectives to describe that feeling would be ominous, foreboding, fearful, anxious, uncomfortable, and repulsive.

As mentioned, I felt the energy shift as soon as it left our physical space. The energetic dissonance between my ***energetic vibration*** and that of the entity is what I picked up on.

Bedtime Example

In another example, one night several years ago I was sleeping soundly when I awoke with a start. I felt the energy in our bedroom had significantly dropped. Looking around for what was happening, I identified there were two powerful dark entities just inside our bedroom door.

I asked for them to be removed from our space and the

energy shifted, feeling better immediately. I was able to go back to sleep within just a few minutes without issue.

This is another example of energetic dissonance. Due to my personal awareness, the literal feeling of the heavier energy compared to my own was what awakened me.

Developing Awareness

Many years ago now, but at the time early on my path of spiritual growth and development, I decided it was more important to feel good than to satisfy what I perceived to be my responsibilities and obligations, mostly about our business.

Historically, I was in a habit of arriving to our shop early and leaving late just so that I knew everything was accomplished for the day. It was quite a shift for me to start taking the time to become "aware" and to connect with The Universe every morning prior to going to the shop.

I decided to ignore that nagging feeling of responsibility. At the time, working harder certainly wasn't working for me. I now know taking the time to connect and to become "aware" not only helped me personally, but played a major role in turning our company around as well.

I started my connection practice at the time I was learning to resolve *trapped energies,* as I described when working with Paul and Alice. So it was normal for me to begin by first noticing how I was feeling in my body.

If I felt something uncomfortable I would resolve the issue(s) just because I would feel better. This practice has continued to help me to maintain a clean *energy body*. And I am now able to notice quickly when my equilibrium is upset.

My hour each morning became a cherished time. When driving, I would listen to "spiritual" authors. I heard Eckhart Tolle mention "*meditation*" one day, so I added that to my morning routine. I didn't have any idea about what I was doing. But I learned to essentially become the observer of thoughts that over a fairly short time led to having less thoughts and quieting my mind.

I noticed that as I did this, I would experience a feeling of elation. The thoughts in my head were no longer clouding my experience. This led to having direct experiences with my **Spirit Team,** to whom I am so grateful.

I continue to take time to connect. During the day's activities, I maintain kind of an ongoing self-check. I've been doing this so long now it's almost an unconscious habit to notice and monitor how I'm feeling moment to moment.

That doesn't mean that I'm impervious to experiencing my own negative or outside heavy energy. It just means I generally do not have to suffer as long as I used to, as I ask for its resolution as soon as it is noticed.

Another way to say this is that now, when I feel heaviness or negative emotion, I'm not taken for an unconscious ride as I react to the uncomfortable feeling(s). Instead, I look at the discomfort with curiosity as an observer. I seek clarity of the root cause with intent to resolve it. Sometimes that includes removing bad guys from my space, aura, or body.

Maintaining a Clean Energy Body

So like maintaining a clean physical body, it is important to maintain a clean energy body. Cleaning energetic debris helps you to maintain your personal "feel good." Maintaining your personal feel good, or high vibration, helps you to quickly recognize any upsets to your equilibrium. Maintaining a clean energy body is an important component to prevention discussed in Chapter Eight.

Learn more about cleaning your energy body in the resources just for you at www.theilluminatedpath.org/unmasked-truth-resources. *Be careful to input the exact address as these resources are otherwise hidden.*

Experiencing Signs & Symptoms

It's important to know that not every feeling in your body is due to the presence of dark energy. As a matter of fact, it is more likely there is a totally different root cause.

We humans can create all sorts of internal energy without the help of bad guy's influence. For instance, the human mind can create all sorts of unpleasant experiences. We can also have trapped emotions, harbor past traumas, have active fears, negative beliefs, and just general negative mind talk. On top of that, we can create subconscious habits that can create and sustain heavy, uncomfortable feelings or energies in the body.

However, should you feel a significant shift from equilibrium, or have other symptoms as described in the previous chapter, it would be prudent to consider if dark energy is either amplifying or is the root cause of the issue.

Additional Methods of Detection

I have hinted at other tools that can be used to corroborate or identify the presence of dark energy. In Chapter One, I talk about working with Paul and Alice. Paul uses **applied kinesiology** or **muscle testing** for guidance.

Muscle Testing

Muscle testing is a technique where the investigator uses the relative weakness or strength of a muscle (typically fingers or an arm) to determine whether a statement is true (a "yes") or not (a "no"). Early on my conscious spiritual path, Paul taught me how to muscle test and I have found it to be very useful.

By using the process of elimination, it is possible to narrow down the root cause of any given issue. Information from other spiritual senses along with muscle testing helps to corroborate the information.

For more on muscle testing, visit the resources available just for you at www.theilluminatedpath.org/unmasked -truth-resources. *Be sure to type in the exact address as these resources are otherwise hidden.*

Spiritual Senses

It's also possible to use spiritual senses similar to Alice to receive information. Alice uses **clairvoyance** (clear sight) among other things to receive guidance and information. Her ability to see the non-physical in such detail is astonishing. In the case of dark energy, it is hard to fool someone who is able to perceive and look directly at it.

Energetic dissonance is felt using **clairsentience**, or "clear feeling." You may also receive supporting information as "clear knowing," **claircognizance,** or "clear hearing," **clairaudients**.

While not specifically the subject of this book, everyone has and can develop their spiritual senses. It is just a matter of exploring what is natural for you, having the intent to develop them and practicing.

Pendulum

A *pendulum* is a tool that can also be used to receive "yes" and "no" answers, much like muscle testing. Again, by using the process of elimination it is possible to determine the root causes of issues.

Loved Ones

As discussed, loved ones can also help you detect dark energy. My wife has now had enough experience that if she notices I'm feeling off she'll ask me, "You got a bug?" There are times I'll have missed a subtle influence.

Back in the beginning when these guys used to "hit me," it was the "big bad guys" that would try to influence me in one way or another. Due to their powerful, uncomfortable repulsive energy, I quickly learned to identify, avoid, and/or remove them.

As mentioned earlier, their tactic seems to have changed with me. "They," (my perception is these guys are being directed) will send in very little guys into my energy field or body. The little guys are barely perceptible. That has helped hone my awareness to these lower-level bad guys.

Chapter Summary

Bad guys can be detected by maintaining awareness and noticing dissonance in your equilibrium. Having a cleansing practice will allow you to continuously monitor your physical body and environment for uncomfortable energy that could be associated with bad guys. Using other tools or spiritual gifts will help to confirm the root cause of any specific energy.

CHAPTER SEVEN

REMOVAL

I believe that dark energy's detection *and removal* has historically been perceived as something quite difficult to accomplish. In reality, from my experience, it is actually quite easy. Removal of dark energy from one's space, energetic field, or body is as easy as identifying it, asking for its removal, then monitoring to confirm improvement or removal.

You now know how to identify a dark entity based on symptoms and your awareness. But who do we ask for help? Well, based on previous examples you probably know, it is Archangel Michael.

Spiritual Support Team

Since you are on a conscious spiritual path, you likely know that each of us has a spiritual support team. For instance, each of us has a guardian angel that protects us for life. There are also archangels who it seems from my experience fill a more specialized role. At the risk of way overgeneralizing, among the many archangels, Archangel Michael is known as our protector, Archangel Gabriel helps with communication, while Archangel Raphael helps with healing.

Guides can help with any human undertaking; guides have generally been physical prior to becoming a guide. I have an incredible business guide that I work with often for example. Some loved ones who have crossed over may even play a role. I know that my father is on my team for instance. And then there are Masters like Jesus or The Buddha, among many others, who can and will work with us, not to mention God, Source, or the Creator. They are all real!

If you haven't had a direct experience with your team, you can do it now! Check out "Experience Your Team" in the resources available just for you at www.theilluminatedpath.org/unmasked-truth-resources. *Be sure to input the exact address as these resources are otherwise hidden.*

Asking for Removal

If you were brought up in a Christian religion like me, you may be surprised that Jesus isn't the "go to" helper when it comes to removal. He is certainly well versed in the "problem" and I do call on him when I feel added help is necessary. But in my experience, your single most beneficial helper when it comes to dark energy removal is Archangel Michael.

As mentioned, he is our protector angel and is very powerful. From my experience, there is not anything that he can't clear or remove. However, there are a few things that Archangel Michael needs in order to assist you.

The first we have covered in-depth. He needs to know where the assistance is needed. As mentioned in Chapter One, due to the vibrational difference between Archangel Michael, (actually all in The Light), and the dark entity, he may not be able to see it without the guidance on where to look. Checking with a muscle test, this seems this is true 80 percent of the time.

Therefore, we need to be able to detect where the energy is residing. Again, it could be in our space (house, office, car, etc.), in our aura, or within our body.

As you practice awareness, you will find you are able to pinpoint where the uncomfortable energy is residing. You just need to focus on it to determine its location. This is opposed to only noticing you don't feel good while not taking the time to focus your attention to determine "why."

So once you notice an upset, you need to go deeper to determine where the uncomfortable energy is coming from. Is it an area outside of your body? Does it seem to be in your environment or does it seem like it is closer to you, perhaps within your aura? Do you notice an uncomfortable sensation anywhere in your body? It could be anywhere, but typical areas are heart, stomach, head, throat, and shoulders. Once you have the location at least generally defined, you are ready to proceed.

Next it is necessary to ask for Archangel Michael's help! Due to the **Law of Free Will**, no one from Love and Light will act on your behalf without your express consent! (This was news to me when I first started on my spiritual path! I thought I was protected and assisted automatically. Not so.) However, simply asking for help will begin the process.

Let's create an example. Let's pretend that you have identified an uncomfortable disturbance in your vibration based on the criteria that we have outlined thus far. Today, something mildly angered you, but now you are noticing that the feeling seems to persist. (You have noticed the general condition.)

You take a minute to look with curiosity into what is going on. You notice that you have tightness in your throat and your heart seems to ache. It wasn't like that this morning when you left for work. You seem more and more irritable as the day progresses.

Finally, you decide that it doesn't hurt to ask Archangel Michael to look at this potential issue for you. (You can ask for help as formally or informally as feels natural for you. I tend to be informal. I feel like it's just asking a friend for a hand.) So you continue . . .

"Archangel Michael, can you take a look at my throat/heart area? I feel like I may have a bad guy. Please remove it if you see anything." I sometimes even point to the area where I am feeling the disturbance as I ask for removal.

Now don't just ask and then move on with your day. Take the time to monitor the area to see if you notice a shift or resolution of the feeling. Generally I feel the relief quite rapidly; like within thirty seconds. However, when helping others I have found it can take longer, minutes to a few hours.

Either way, the resolution of the negative feeling is your confirmation that the entity has been removed and "apprehended." Of course, Archangel Michael will encourage it to return to The Light or will place it in "holding." More on this shortly. With focus, you may be able to confirm this with your other spiritual senses or tools as well.

Gratitude

I always thank Archangel Michael, Jesus, and whoever else may be involved on my team with heart-felt gratitude. Gratitude is good for you as it just feels good, but also confirms to your spiritual team that they have adequately accomplished what you have requested and it was what you desired.

Control Device/Implant Removal

If you suspect a control device or implant, you can follow the same steps as above; just ask Archangel Michael for his help removing/resolving the issue, then point (either in your mind or literally) to where the problem area is. Then watch for the relief and end with gratitude.

Partial/No Resolution

There are times that I have to ask for help a second or third time because I am feeling only partial or no resolution to the issue.

If this is the case, my follow up conversation with Archangel Michael usually is something like, "I felt some relief Archangel Michael, but I feel like there is still another 50 percent remaining in that same area. Can you take another look please?" (Many times, I'll physically point to the area I'm feeling the greatest upset.)

The reason you may not feel full resolution the first time is there can be more than one entity involved. In my experience, "bigger" or more powerful bad guys generally work alone, but sometimes they can have "minions" that they direct.

Minions Example

A short time ago, I was called on to determine the cause of a client's anger and sadness. This person said they were crying all the time and felt like they just, "didn't want to go on."

I was surprised, as this person is generally very upbeat. I checked her energetic vibration on a scale of one to nineteen, nineteen being the lowest, correlating with shame and humiliation. She had fallen to a seven (neutrality) within an hour. She typically was between a one (peace) and three (love) on this scale so the drop was quite significant in a short time.

I checked the root cause of the issue and found there to be a fairly large bad guy in this person's aura around her heart. On the scale of one to ten, ten being highest level of power, this bad guy was a 7.4.

I asked Archangel Michael to remove this entity and confirmed it had occurred. I checked to see if this person was feeling the relief and while she wasn't at that moment, my muscle testing indicated she would in about fifteen minutes. Fifteen minutes passed and my client indicated they were indeed feeling somewhat better, but still felt the issue wasn't fully resolved.

I continued to check for the root cause of a potential secondary issue and another bad guy was found that was a level 5.3 out of 10. I asked for removal and this person experienced full resolution momentarily. These two bad guys cumulative power was quite significant, the reason this person's vibration was dropping so quickly and why she was feeling like she just, "didn't want to go on," in her words. I confirmed this secondary entity was a minion of the first.

After removal of both of these bad guys, my client's energetic vibration returned to a one (peace) and I could both feel the shift and see the improvement in her overall demeanor. Her spirit had literally lightened as she returned to her normal equilibrium.

While there can even be multiple minions involved, in my experience, minions being directed by larger (more powerful) bad guys is relatively rare.

Multiple Small Guys

More often, if there are multiple entities, it is the less powerful "little" bad guys who inhabit the same space. I mentioned earlier that I have found, relatively recently, their new tactic with me is to send multiple little bad guys to create the upset as opposed to one more powerful (more detectable) entity. The less powerful bad guys are more difficult to detect because the negative feeling from them is less noticeable. (Their vibration is not as noticeably overwhelming as the more powerful entities.)

As mentioned in Chapter One, bad guys working together have a cumulative effect. That is if there is a "level two" (little) bad guy working with a "level three" (little) bad guy, their cumulative energy or effect is as though you have a "level five" mid-level bad guy creating the disturbance or influence.

Hidden/Masked Revisited

In Chapter Three, Tactics, I mention that at least some dark entities have the ability to hide or "mask" themselves. So even though you have pinpointed the exact area of concern (by noticing the symptoms and using your awareness and other spiritual senses) even pointing right to the problem area, Archangel Michael sometimes will not be able to see it because the entity is hidden and/or masked. Checking quickly with a muscle test, this happens about 23 percent of the time, almost a quarter.

So if on the second try you still do not experience relief, then ask Archangel Michael to check "hidden or masked." I mentioned in Chapter Three just by checking "hidden or masked," it is like the hiding spot is revealed or the masking is removed. I frankly have no idea why, other than perhaps it's a Universal Law that must be followed, but again, this is total speculation. For us, it is just important to know that it works.

There is one final thing to note regarding the feeling of resolution or relief. While for me it is typical to feel a shift within thirty seconds, I have worked with others and found it can take ten to fifteen minutes or even a few hours to feel full relief. It is likely different for everyone.

So if you don't feel resolution in the moment and you feel you have adequately identified where the issue is located and asked for Archangel Michael's help, then pay attention over the next minutes to hours to see if there is a more gradual resolution. You may even feel partial relief that continues to full relief over time.

Using Your Spiritual Senses & Tools

Non-physical bad guys have an advantage compared to us physical 3D humans. Generally speaking, it seems to me that unaware humans are like sitting ducks. We have no idea they are around or a potential bother; one of the big reasons for this book.

As we have already discussed, using your personal awareness helps to even the playing field. Even better is when you utilize your other supportive spiritual senses.

As you focus on "problem areas," you may find you receive other "spiritual" or "non-physical" information supporting whatever you are focused on.

In Chapter Two, I described the experience of my wife sobbing as she slept in our bed and how I totally saw (in my mind's eye) a little bad guy jumping up and down on her shoulders. In this case, my wife didn't have to pinpoint the location of where she was feeling the upset as I could see where the problem was originating from and directed Archangel Michael based on that information.

Similarly, I described how Alice receives information through "spiritual sight" or clairvoyance. Yet her other senses (feeling, knowing, and even smelling) are active. Supporting information supplied by your other spiritual senses is very helpful.

You can also develop "spiritual tools" such as applied kinesiology (muscle testing) or use a pendulum to receive validating information as mentioned earlier.

Keep in mind that muscle testing can be interrupted by the bad guys. Also, if the person doing the muscle testing is emotionally engaged in the question or situation, the muscle tests may not be reliable. Checking on my specific accuracy of muscle testing for the purpose of identifying dark energy, my muscle test indicates it is about 87 percent reliable. However, this likely varies by person and experience level. So other corroborating information is very helpful to confirm any given situation.

When working with my Team for myself or working with a client, I generally confirm the source of the sensations I receive with a muscle test. Similar to Alice, I have also found when tuning into another's energy I can feel where the area of concern is located. Again, I generally confirm these feelings with a muscle test.

Helpful, Not Mandatory

While it's certainly helpful and nice to have the corroborating evidence from other spiritual senses, it's not mandatory for resolution. Just focusing on the feeling and experiencing the resolution is enough.

I have confirmed this approach a number of times by only using awareness without corroborating information from other non-physical senses or muscle testing. Over the last several months, when I have felt I have had a bad guy influence, I have simply pinpointed the location or source of it, asked Archangel Michael for help removing it, and then monitored to assure its resolution.

Each time I experienced 100 percent relief. I then went back to confirm the root cause and in those cases each time a dark entity was the influence. These happened to be smaller, less powerful bad guys. But that indicates the larger bad guys would be even easier to notice.

I also described a time early on my path when I was feeling like I was being "attacked" during a drive home. I called on Archangel Michael and experienced full resolution with no corroborating information then too. The point is, as long as you are aware, you can resolve these issues!

Having the additional spiritual/non-physical tools at your disposal allows for deeper understanding while resolving issues at a finer level. With practice, your non-physical/spiritual senses will naturally develop further if they are not developed already.

Bad Guys Aren't Destroyed

Archangel Michael can remove dark entities from a human's aura or body because the bad guys are breaking Universal Law. Dark entities seek to influence humans violating their free will and are uninvited guests whether they are just reaching into our energy body or if they fully enter into our aura or physical body.

Early along my path, I remember being so surprised and frankly miffed that the dark entities were not destroyed after wreaking so much havoc. My ego really wanted justice. Yet, I was taught about unconditional Love.

My understanding about what happens to dark entities once they are removed comes from working with Paul and Alice and Alice's description(s) each time one would be removed from me.

Alice would describe how Archangel Michael, and sometimes Jesus (and others), would talk to the removed (caught) entity and encourage them to return to The Light. I don't remember any returning to The Light.

Over the years, I have consistently checked to see if those that I had identified (and Archangel Michael removed) returned to The Light and the answer was always, "no," so I finally stopped checking.

When the entity didn't go to The Light, Alice described how they were put into a white box or holding cell of sorts. They would be left there but would be checked on periodically to see if they had a change of heart. However, while there, they would not be able to harm anyone; they were inert. Perhaps this is the reason for the concept of purgatory.

It occurred to me to check to see if any of those that were put into a white box / holding cell since I started having these experiences had yet returned to The Light. (This would be since 2007.) I feel I've identified and Archangel Michael has removed hundreds from me and others during this time.

Checking with a muscle test, I'm pleasantly surprised. Over the last fifteen years, at least twenty-six have returned to The Light. That is a small percentage, but better than zero!

Helping Others

We have been talking about removal of dark energies from our personal environment, energy, or physical body. However, as you become more experienced you may wish to assist others. Frankly, I had a bit of a bumpy start when I started trying to assist others to the point my team, especially Jesus and Archangel Michael, told me to stop. I wasn't helping and was potentially making things worse!

I did stop and even then I was continually reminded not to do anything. This was actually the most direct and urgent guidance I have ever received from them. It is extremely rare to be "told" what is in the best interest due to free will. However, at this point they knew my heart and that I meant well, but at that time I simply didn't have enough experience to be helpful.

I did continue to work on myself, however. Ever so gradually, opportunities arose to help others. So the nuances are important to know prior to being effective helping others.

Full Awareness

Talking with Archangel Michael and Jesus through Alice, we checked on the question: Is it helpful to remove bad guys that had been identified, (like in a loved one), without their knowledge?

The answer was that there are a couple issues with that. First, if a bad guy is removed without a person's full awareness, chances are good another same size or even bigger entity will fill the void within that person potentially causing worse issues. So, any time an entity is removed it needs to be with full awareness of the person involved. Secondly, there is the ethical issue of working within someone's energy body without their full knowledge.

There is one exception to this "permission" rule. Young children, generally under the age of seven who are fully dependent on their parents or caregivers, with the permission of the parent or caregiver, may give permission for the child. However, there is an age range based on the maturity of the child and it should be confirmed with intuitive guidance or other spiritual tools prior to proceeding.

Permission is not required to clear free space, and it may be performed at any time. Space clearing is discussed more in the next chapter.

Let Archangel Michael Do the Work

Recently I was listening to a spiritual/life coach who was sharing about how she had been working with a client who was feeling bad. They identified "an energy," and the coach's understanding was to "send the energy back to where it came from." In this case, the energy was returned to the client's father. This coach explained that within two days of this experience, the father had taken his own life.

This poignant example demonstrates why it is best to allow Archangel Michael to do all of the work when it comes to removal and disposition of bad guys. It assures that it is done safely, that the bad guy(s) are actually "apprehended" and not just redirected, and it releases you from this responsibility.

I Didn't Feel Anything

It is important to remember that not everything that we experience that is uncomfortable is due to a bad guy.

As mentioned earlier, our human mind and our focus are very powerful. We can create all kinds of fears, difficulties, bad feelings, and experiences and generally have a lower energetic vibration or state-of-being just by what we are focused on.

Additionally, there can be other energetic influences that can create similar internal energy as what is experienced with bad guys. Trapped emotions from past traumas can become active, along with unhelpful subconscious program(s), energetic cords, an out of balance chakra energy system, a dirty auric field, and even diet can create similar uncomfortable feeling(s) like those associated with a bad guy.

However, from my experience these other energy types described above remain relatively constant over time. Also, there is not the additional feeling of foreboding, repulsion, or ominousness.

Just remember, if you don't feel relief it is possible there is another energetic root cause.

Additional Assistance

By maintaining a clear *energy body*, it is possible to maintain a general "feel good." By feeling good, it is much easier to determine when an upset is experienced. If you would like assistance with clearing your energy body, see the resources available just for you at www.theilluminatedpath.org/ unmasked-truth-resources. *Be sure to type in the exact address as these resources are otherwise hidden.*

If you would like personal help clearing your energy body or with the identification and removal of dark energy, visit www.theilluminatedpath.org/support.

Chapter Summary

Removal is accomplished quite simply by identifying the dark energy based on observation of your symptoms and looking deeper and finding the location of the upset. Next you have to ask Archangel Michael to look into the affected area to remove the bad guy if one is present, remembering to ask him to also check "hidden or masked," especially if resolution isn't experienced. When relief is felt, sending heart-felt gratitude for the assistance helps him to know his assistance was effective while confirming it was what was desired.

CHAPTER EIGHT

PREVENTION & PROTECTION

High Vibration

One of the best methods to minimize the impact of dark entities on your life is to maintain a high vibration; to generally feel good.

Bad guys are not an energetic match to high vibration. By definition they are (at least currently) lower vibrational beings. Therefore, by maintaining higher vibration, there is natural protection.

Also, by feeling good it is possible to quickly identify when there is an upset to your equilibrium. It is much more difficult to notice these influences when feeling bad or having strong negative emotional experiences.

An enormous side benefit to feeling good is that the Law of Attraction brings you more "feel good." I often tell folks I work with that, "feeling good is the most important thing."

When feeling good is truly your most important desire, you choose differently. Perhaps you decide not to argue, call others names, compare yourself, choose anger, seek vengeance, or any other typical, negative human behavior.

Instead, you look deeper into your own psyche for the root cause of not feeling good. Each of us has natural Peace. It is just covered up by years of accumulated heavier energy. By resolving those issues, it is very possible to experience Peace as your default state-of-being.

For more resources on establishing and maintaining your personal "feel good" or high vibration, visit www. theilluminatedpath.org/unmasked-truth-resources. *Be sure to type in the exact address as the resources are otherwise hidden.*

Strong Intent

Having strong intent that you will not tolerate bad guy's behavior is also effective. The overall feeling of, "NO, YOU ARE NOT WELCOME HERE. I AM NOT PLAYING."

Alice has described for me, on several occasions, identifying bad guys in her environment and escorting them off the premises with her intent.

Personal Space

Bad guys will frequent where there is opportunity. That includes areas of higher traffic.

Therefore, when going into public areas, stores, events, movies, etc., I have gotten into the habit of asking for an energetic bubble of high vibration around my personal space before entering the venue.

I do this with my personal intent and imagination. My intent is that I'm drawing upon Universal Love and Light energy to create this energetic sphere.

When doing this, I stop for just a brief moment, take a deep breath, and say, "please surround me with Love, Light and protection." When I say the word "protection" I breathe out rapidly and see "in my mind's eye" an energetic explosion of Light. It is like a bright star exploding within and then flowing outward to create a sphere of high vibrational Love and Light.

My intent is to make the sphere "the ideal size." However, you can determine the size created if you desire. Additionally, my intent is for anything not matching the high vibration sphere to "bounce off" and not bother me.

There are a few things to remember. The Love and Light sphere, or bubble, needs to be renewed every two and a half to three hours, as the energy created dissipates over time.

Another important thing to remember is if you lower your vibration for whatever reason, perhaps getting angry or frustrated, the protection sphere will shatter because it is not a vibrational match.

Finally, while the sphere of Love and Light is helpful, I have experienced bad guys breaching it either by entering my personal space or using an energetic device. The example of the energetic spear in my knee at the gym was one such experience.

Checking with a muscle test, it prevents around 80 percent of the potential issues, so a fairly high percentage. So while it is not foolproof, I feel it also reinforces my personal focus and strong intent ahead of time. This is opposed to being taken off guard.

You can also ask Archangel Michael to clear your physical space at the same time you perform the above procedure if desired. This just provides additional assurance if you feel it is needed.

Avoiding Environments

When traveling, us humans know to avoid areas that may experience higher frequency of traffic incidents or crime. We seek to stay clear of the problem areas to minimize potential issues.

Well, the same is helpful when minimizing bad guy's impact on our lives. I have found it is important to be discerning.

For instance, if I walk into an establishment and the environment doesn't "feel good," I will leave. If I have to stay for some reason, I ask to be surrounded by Love and Light as just described and ask that angels "stand watch" for added awareness. (The intent is that the angels nudge me if I'm missing anything.)

This isn't out of fear, as I know it is simple to remove any influence that may be encountered. It just wastes less time and minimizes grief by avoiding issues.

Finally, horror movies are always avoided. Fear is a great entry point for bad guys to mask themselves. The themes of these films are not rooted in Love and Light and so I avoid them.

Clearing Physical Environments

Physical space can also be cleared of any lower vibrational energies, whether it be bad guys, *psychic radiations,* or thought forms as mentioned earlier.

This can actually be accomplished with one's own awareness, if desired, while working together with Archangel Michael. Very much like clearing a bad guy from your aura or body, you can identify dark energy using your spiritual senses or tools and then ask for Archangel Michael to escort them from the premises. I actually used to clear space this way.

Another way to clear space is by *saging.* Saging is accomplished by using a "smudge stick," or bundle of sage, that is burned over an ashtray and the resulting smoke directed to the area(s) in the environment where clearing is desired. You can sage rooms in your house by directing the smoke into the area desired with the intent that that area be cleared.

Very similar to other methods, saging likely works due to the focused intent. I have never personally saged, yet I have respected friends that utilize this method routinely.

Yet I feel the most efficient method for clearing space is simply asking for it. It takes much less time. Asking for assistance also allows us to continue to grow our relationship with our **Spirit Team**.

Space Clearing Experience

Just a few days ago (at the time of writing this book,) I had been out and about doing errands. I worked in my home office for a few hours, had dinner, and then began to wind down for the evening.

I went to our garage (where we keep our drinks) and noticed that familiar, ominous, foreboding feeling. I didn't even check to see if this was a bad guy as I had a "knowing" based on experience. (It's possible this entity followed me home from running errands or was wandering through the neighborhood.)

Immediately, I asked Archangel Michael to do a "sweep" of our garage and entire house. I waited to notice the shift and after a few moments all felt calm and peaceful again.

I went inside and found after a few moments the feeling returned. I was surprised it wasn't completely resolved. So I continued to "watch," mostly using feeling. I then asked for a clearing again, but this time also asked that Archangel Michael stand right next to me.

I know that he did, because as soon as I asked I felt my immediate environment return to peace and calm. I asked him to stand with me for ten minutes as I continued to "watch."

After ten minutes, I checked our house environment confirming all was clear using a muscle test, and it was confirmed. I thanked Archangel Michael for his help and faithfulness and carried on the evening without further issue.

Angels Stand Watch

Once your space is cleared, as mentioned earlier, I have also found it helpful to ask for angels to "stand watch" as well. I use this mostly when going to sleep but have also used it with clients if it seems that it would be helpful.

Every night before going to bed, I ask for our house to be cleared, I then surround it with Love, Light, and protection, just like when doing so with personal space. I then ask for angels to "please stand watch."

If you ask angels to stand watch, see if you can notice where they are at after you have asked for assistance. You may feel them, see them, have an impression of them, and perhaps even hear them. Ultimately it feels good and is comforting. I usually get an impression of two angels standing watch on either side of the foot of our bed.

Revisiting Bedtime Example

In Chapter Six, I shared an example of using awareness to identify two bad guys in our environment when I awoke with a start from a sound sleep.

Later, I explored this situation with Alice and my Team. The previous night I had asked angels to stand watch and felt confident they were with me. I wondered how then I could have had two big bad guys in our bedroom and they didn't do anything about it.

The answer from the angels was that there wasn't any threat. The bad guys were just "passing through." I then realized I failed to set the intent that I wished for any bad guys to be escorted from our environment, not just if they were going to "do something." Lesson learned; it is important to be specific.

Jesus

I'd also like to revisit my experience from Chapter One when I was working with Paul and Alice. You recall Alice watched as Jesus stood between me and a big bad guy.

I bring this up as Jesus is obviously in tune with our earthly realities. He can assist and call in whoever is necessary should additional help be necessary.

However, over the years, it has seemed like more times than not Jesus has deferred to Archangel Michael since this is his specialty.

Note: Other Masters are likely also very helpful. I'm just mentioning Jesus here because of our relationship.

Free Space

Keep in mind space not occupied by humans is considered "free space." Dark entities are free to roam free space. When clearing your personal space or environment, the intent is to move entities away to free space while maintaining the sovereignty of your personal environment.

Thinking about Them

When first becoming a target to these entities, I mentioned how I found it difficult to discipline my mind and not "look" for them all of the time. Soon I found that the very act of looking for them was creating an opening.

It seems our personal focus is very powerful in The Universe and the same holds true on this subject. Therefore, in order to minimize this issue, maintain your awareness and just "be the observer."

While it is helpful to notice if you are being bothered by a bad guy while taking steps to remove their impact, obsessing about them is not helpful.

Chapter Summary

To minimize bad guy's potential influence, maintain a personal high vibration (or feel good) and strong personal intent. Routinely clear your personal space. Clear your home or other personal environment by asking Archangel Michael to clear it or using another method. When in public or less than ideal environments, ask to surround your personal space with a Love, Light, and protection sphere and ask for angels to stand watch for additional assistance. Finally, be discerning about the environments you frequent and be the observer as opposed to obsessively thinking about bad guys.

CHAPTER NINE

ENCOURAGEMENT

I Know—Righteous Indignation

As you know, when I first learned about the real existence of bad guys I was quite (what I felt to be) righteously indignant to say the least. I couldn't believe that we had invisible beings that were actively seeking to dissuade us however they could.

You Have the Power

However, over time I have come to accept this reality as part of our existence here on the earth plane. Just like any other obstacle we face, it is possible to learn to navigate this issue with confident ability. You have the power! The secret is maintaining your own personal awareness. By doing so, it is easy to identify upsets to your equilibrium.

Love & Light

Love and Light energy are infinitely more powerful than the heavy dark energy these beings embody. They actually still have a spark of Light within them. They just have removed themselves from The Light so considerably that their behavior becomes grotesque. They simply have lost their way.

While I understand the indignation that can be experienced, I now view these beings with compassion. I actually feel bad that they have lost their way so significantly. I do hope that each may find their way Home again into the Unconditional Love offered to all of us by our Source.

Each so called "bad guy" that we identify and that is removed (by Archangel Michael) has the option to return to The Light. If they do not wish to return to The Light, they are "held" and checked on from time to time. Either way, our world becomes brighter as they are not able to negatively influence others again.

Your Spirit Team

You can trust your Spirit Team to assist you. Your trust is not misplaced. I work with my Team daily. I'm so thankful to have them to lean on for assistance with all of my earthly needs and desires.

As mentioned multiple times, Archangel Michael is very powerful and is always willing to help. Remember, you have to ask. He and others from The Light will not act without asking due to the Law of Free Will.

By working with your Team for this or any reason, you develop a deeper relationship with them. I now think of my

Spirit Team as my best friends. I'm so thankful for their genuine interest in and faithfulness to me. Their deep Love is felt and certainly reciprocated. If you didn't already know, your Team feels the exact same way about you. It is worth the effort to develop your relationship with them.

Develop Skills

With the knowledge contained in this book, it is possible to develop your own set of skills to enable you to identify the energetic signature of these beings and thus avoid, clear, or remove them. I have shared examples and offered how my awareness picks up on bad guys in my environment, aura, or body.

It is possible you will become aware of them differently. For instance, I mention that I use muscle testing to confirm the other intuitive information that I receive. However, there are some who find that they do not resonate with this tool.

As you learn how you best connect with the nonphysical, it will help you to hone your skills and abilities. However it works for you is what is most important; not trying to "do it" in a way someone else suggests if it doesn't resonate with you.

However, the information in this book can help you to determine if what is being experienced is due to bad-guy influence.

Connecting & Your Intent

I am encouraging you to connect with your non-physical Spirit Team. But you may be wondering how to connect with just the

Good Guys (your Spirit Team from Love & Light), and how to avoid connecting or attracting the bad guys.

It's all based on your intent. Having the clear intent to only connect with The Light is the key. By maintaining this intent, you will indeed connect only with beings from The Light.

Added Assistance

From my experience, I have found it to be very helpful to have added support from others who have already developed the skills needed to navigate this issue. If you feel you or someone you know could benefit from additional help, you can find assistance at www.theilluminatedpath.org/support or www. richhamm.com.

Join The Army of Light, a Force For Good!

Would you like to join The Army of Light, a Force for Good?

First know that being part of The Army of Light is about your personal intent and depth of conviction. It's about doing all you can to let your Light shine and to spread Light in our world. This is a personal covenant you make with The Universe on your own. (This may already be your focus!)

Since we know that anything that is resisted persists, The Army of Light does not oppose darkness; it promotes The Light. The shield is used to deflect upsets when necessary, but the Sword of Light cuts through darkness as Truth is sought, illuminating not only ours but other's paths.

By joining together, The Army becomes an even stronger force for Good. This is due to the cumulative energetic power of The Army's focus. "When two or three are gathered together, I will be in the midst of you." When even more are gathered, more collective positive energy helps to shift the world we live in! It literally becomes "a force."

You can join The Army of Light with your heartfelt intent. Simply decide and lead with that conviction moment by moment, day by day.

The Army of Light at The Illuminated Path

There is something else you can do as a member of The Army of Light if it resonates with you. In our world today, the reason that books get published and influencers become household names is due to the size of their platforms.

A platform is another word for a group of followers; the larger the number, the larger the platform. By subscribing to The Illuminated Path's email list, our platform grows. When our platform grows, more opportunities arise to extend our reach, spreading Light in the world. We would be honored to have you as part of The Army of Light at The Illuminated Path! You can subscribe at www.theilluminatedpath.org/contact-subscribe.

Another very helpful way to spread The Light is to offer an honest review of this book online. Reviewing this book provides credibility so that other potential readers have confidence in its contents. It is our goal for this book to sell well, not because it is our desire to be in the spotlight, but so that our cumulative Light can shine brighter.

My Deepest Love

Whether or not you visit the website, subscribe to the email list, or offer a book review, know that I am honored to be on "The Path" with you! I am so grateful that you have read this book. I trust that you have found it illuminating and that the Truth has been Unmasked.

You totally got this! I send my deepest love as you continue to navigate this great adventure! Here we go! Woo-hoo!

THE
ILLUMINATED
PATH

FREE READER RESOURCES

As an exclusive special gift for readers of this book, I have created a private, readers-only page at The Illuminated Path where you can:

- **Learn How To Become Aware**
- **Learn How To Clean Your Energy Body**
- **Experience Your Spirit Team**
- **Learn About Muscle Testing**
- **Access A Link For Personal Assistance**

THE
ILLUMINATED PATH

VISIT

www.theilluminatedpath.org/unmasked-truth-resources

GLOSSARY

The following definitions are based on my usage, understanding, and meaning of the words or phrases. Most are not dictionary definitions and also may or may not reflect the same meaning(s) as used by other authors or teachers.

Applied Kinesiology: Applied Kinesiology, also known as "muscle testing," is a tool that can be developed and utilized to receive intuitive information. Making a statement, then performing a muscle test, indicates the truth or falsehood of the statement. This is done by measuring the relative strength, (a "yes) or weakness, (a "no") of the muscle. See more about muscle testing at www.theilluminatedpath.org/unmasked-truth-resources.

Aura: The aura is the invisible energy field that extends outward and surrounds a person's physical body.

Auric Field: See Aura.

Bad Guys: One descriptive term for "demons" or dark entities. The following terms are used interchangeably in this book: *Dark Energy, Demons, Bad Guys, Dark Entities, Entity or Entities.*

Chakra Energy System: Non-physical energy centers in the body that affect your physical and emotional well-being.

Clairaudient: Clear Hearing; A non-physical sense where a person feels like they intuitively "hear." About 6 percent of the population experience clairaudience *based on a muscle test.*

Claircognizant: Clear Knowing; A non-physical sense where the person feels like they intuitively "know." About 22 percent of the population experience claircognizance *based on a muscle test.*

Clairsentient: Clear Feeling; A non-physical sense where the person intuitively "feels" energy. About 93 percent of the population experience clairsentience *based on a muscle test.*

Clairvoyant: Clear Sight; a non-physical sense where the person receives intuitive information through impressions, images, and/or movies. About 40 percent of the population experience some form of clairvoyance *based on a muscle test.*

Conscious Spiritual Path: We are all on a "spiritual path" even if we are unaware of it. However, this is my term for being aware or knowing about being on a spiritual path.

Dark Energy: One descriptive term for "demons" or dark entities. The following terms are used interchangeably in this book: *Dark Energy, Demons, Bad Guys, Dark Entities, Entity or Entities*.

Dracula: The main vampire character in Bram Stoker's horror novel that later became the basis for a whole genre of literature, film, and animation. Dracula wore a cape similar to those worn by powerful dark entities.

Drive-Bys: My slang term for when I would feel "attacked" by one or more dark entities. These happened so often (several per day for at least five years), I needed a term to identify the experience to my life/spiritual development coaches.

Earth-Bound Spirit: An earth-bound spirit is a deceased human whose spirit has been released from his body but for some reason hasn't returned Home or crossed over back to The Light.

From my understanding, there are a number of reasons this may happen. After physical death, the being may not know to look for or to follow The Light, it may not fully know it is deceased, it may not want to leave the earth plane so it can remain and protect a person or a place, or it could be focused on an aspect of their earth plane life that they wish to continue experiencing like alcohol, drugs, or sex to name a few.

Earth-bound spirits can also attach to physical humans. They can have similar effects as dark entities in that they can encourage bad behavior and drain the energy of the person they have attached to.

Energetic Dissonance: Energetic dissonance is the difference between the vibration of someone who is aware, light, and feeling good compared to the energy of a dark entity that feels heavy, ominous, and foreboding. This energetic difference is felt as a sensation in the body that can alert the aware person to the existence and location of a dark entities.

Energetic Reset: An energetic reset allows the person to re-establish a level of "feel good" that likely isn't routinely experienced. One can achieve an energetic reset by aligning and balancing the chakra energy system, cleansing the auric field, and resolving other energetic disturbances, such as removing dark energies and resolving trapped emotions just to name a few.

Energetic Signature: This is a term I use to describe the feeling of a space or of an entity. There can be a cumulative energetic signature or a singular energetic signature as in how a dark entity feels. However, everything, including inanimate objects, has an energetic signature.

Energetic Vibration: This is a term I use that provides an indication of how someone's spirit is feeling within their body; their personal "feel good" level. This can be measured using a muscle test. The scale I typically use ranges from one to nineteen; one correlating with Peace and nineteen with shame and humiliation. The remaining levels all correlate to a specific feeling tone and can give clear indication of their equilibrium, improvement, or upset.

Energetic Work: This is the action taken to resolve the root cause of non-physical upsets that cause psychological and/or physical discomfort. This can include but is not limited to balancing the chakra energy system, cleansing the aura, releasing conditioning or subconscious programming, resolving trauma, releasing energetic cords, resolving trapped emotions, and removing outside entities to name a few.

Energetically: Non-physical energetic issues. See "energetic work" for more clarity.

Energies: The nonspecific term for a non-physical upset that causes psychological or physical discomfort.

Energy Body: The non-physical aspects of your physical body. By maintaining a clean and clear energy body, natural peace becomes the default state-of-being; it is not covered by energetic debris.

Good Guys: My slang term for those non-physical benevolent beings from The Light.

Higher Self: The concept of the higher self is the view that only a portion of our being is focused into this physical human experience while the vast majority of our being remains non-physically focused in Love and Light. Therefore, our higher self can be called upon for guidance and direction.

Holding Your Center: When holding your center, one becomes the observer in the face of discomfort. The observer is not drawn into the uncomfortable feeling and refrains from putting any kind of meaning or judgement on those sensations or behaviors. For example, "I held my center" as opposed to being "freaked out" by a sensation or behavior.

Holding Your Focus: Holding focus is maintaining concentration on the subject of inquiry.

Intuitive Senses: See Clairaudience, Claircognizance, Clairsentience, and Clairvoyance. Most have a more dominant intuitive sense supported by a secondary sense. However, all intuitive senses can be active as well. Although not mentioned in the body of this book, there are also non-physical senses for smelling, tasting, touch, and empathy (being an empath) as well.

Law of Free Will: Free Will is a fundamental law of The Universe. Source has created each of us in his/her/its image and likeness; we are all creators. Those from The Light will not interfere with another's creation without direct permission. It is a highly regarded principle that is rarely broken.

My understanding is the one exception to this rule is accidents can be prevented from happening without specific permission if the end of that person's incarnation has not arrived.

Maintaining Your Center: See holding your center; the same concept.

Ouija Board: A device used to contact non-physical beings.

Past Life: A concept that we as human spirits have more than one physical lifetime. The idea is trauma(s) can be carried forward into the current lifetime.

Previous Life: See past life. This could also refer to the most recent (past) lifetime.

Psychic Radiations: The non-physical energy emanated from others that can be absorbed by a person.

Saging: The ritual of burning sage or a "smudge stick," sending smoke into the area where clearing is desired.

Spirit Team: The name I have adopted to indicate all of the benevolent spirits from Love and Light who either have considerable interest in or are assigned to us for our development and evolution for our highest and best good. Most humans have many spirits on their Team. They include but are not limited to a guardian angel(s), guides who generally have a specific focus when working with you, and Masters and Archangels to name a few.

Spiritual Surgery: A physical surgery performed by a Spirit or Spirits without the use of physical instruments.

The Universe: The all-encompassing term for "all that is."

Vibration: See Energetic Vibration. Used interchangeably.

ABOUT THE AUTHOR

R ich graduated from Central Michigan University in Mt. Pleasant, Michigan, with a Bachelor of Science in Economics and Management in 1989. He also completed his Private Pilot's license that same year.

Soon after, he earned his Airline Transport Pilot and Flight Instructor certificates, training at several schools, including Spartan School of Aeronautics in Tulsa, Oklahoma, and Andrews University in Berrien Springs, Michigan.

He worked as a corporate pilot until 2002 while performing sales marketing and management roles for those same companies.

However, Rich always felt driven to own his own company. In 2002, he received an offer from the owner of the company he was flying for to become the active principal and general manager for a business that was a "turn around opportunity."

Though reticent, after several weeks of consideration, Rich accepted the offer. He was given ownership stock as "sweat equity" in return. While Rich was concerned about the challenge, he was confident that he could make the enterprise profitable.

However, after several years of trying everything he could think of to turn the business around, the company continued to languish, losing tens of thousands of dollars every month.

So, Rich did something quite surprising. He bought into yet another failing enterprise. His rationale was that he could merge the two companies and ultimately save them both.

However, that plan did not work out well. Both companies continued to lose considerable money over the next two years until finally he received **THE** phone call from his financing partner who said, "I'm not sure what your emergency plan is but you need it now." He had pulled his financial support.

Rich found that he had exhausted himself and all of his options. He was now on the literal brink of personal and financial collapse.

While having some awareness but little real understanding of spiritual laws and principles, Rich found he had nowhere else to turn.

Driving home that fateful day he remembers saying to Jesus, "If you are really there, I could use some help." He was very surprised to feel his anxiety calm immediately, driving home in relative peace. Soon, he was surprised to find his desire to read inspirational books returned.

Rich has since learned how to apply Universal Laws and Spiritual Principles to all areas of his everyday life, including his business, which has led to astonishing experiences and incredible results! Peace is now his default state-of-being, and love, joy, and abundance his common experience.

Rich was able to successfully merge the two companies in 2009, after becoming solidly profitable, and to date has grown their revenue five times with corresponding profitability! Rich remains a principal and runs that same company today.

However, Rich has found a new driving purpose; to share what he has learned with others so that they too may have their own incredible experiences and astonishing results.

Rich has been married to his college sweetheart since 1990. In 2023, his wife retired from being a first-grade teacher. They have two amazing children and live in southwestern Michigan

ACKNOWLEDGMENTS

I would like to thank those who were instrumental in helping this book become fully realized.

My parents, William and Deanna Hamm, and grandparents, Oakley & Irene Best and William & Martha Hamm, provided me with a firm foundation. The lineage of our family seeking depth of understanding is not a mistake. I'm honored to be a part of the Hamm (Best) soul family.

I so appreciate my wife and kids who have lived with me during each stage of my personal growth and development which has not always been smooth. I'm so grateful for your allowing, love and understanding.

My incredible Spirit Team has both taught and led me to each experience for my highest and best good. No words will ever express my heartfelt gratitude, but I know you can feel it. Thank you for your incredible support (putting it mildly) and the opportunity to work together to serve The Kingdom!

The following author's have helped me to better grasp the nature of The Universe and our human experience. I'm deeply appreciative to be a benefactor of your wisdom, Sylvia Browne, Todd Burpo, Jack Canfield, Deepak Chopra, Paulo Coelho, Esther and Jerry Hicks (Abraham), Bruce Lipton,

Anita Moorjani, M. Scott Peck, Don Piper, Agnus Sanford, Eckhart Tolle, James Van Praagh, Neale Donald Walsch, and William Paul Young among many others.

Paul, Alice, and Joy, you helped me to both experience significant energetic shifts, but also to more deeply understand the nature of who we really are. Our experiences over the years have been deeply enlightening and transformative!

Without Alice Brewer's engagement, assistance, suggestions and intuitive guidance throughout this book's creation this project would not have been completed.

There were several who read manuscript drafts. Your suggestions and encouragement gave me the confidence to continue with this project at different but critical and pivotal times. This work would not have been completed without the input of my wife Becky, brothers Don and Jeff Hamm, Uncle Brewster (Buck) Hamm, Joy, and my good buddy Nenad Nikolic.

Those at The Illuminated Path who voted on various aspects of this book, including the book's cover design (assuring its broadest appeal) were incredibly helpful, thank you!

MayFly Design made this book better in all ways. Thank you, Sean Micheal Strain for your editing and support, Molly Mortimer for your incredible book design work, and Julie and Ryan Scheife for your oversight, administration, and your assistance in making this book available and marketable. I can't speak highly enough about your care, quality, professionalism, and attention to detail. Thank you sincerely.